*Curiosities Series*

# MICHIGAN
## *Curiosities*

### QUIRKY CHARACTERS,
### ROADSIDE ODDITIES & OTHER
### OFFBEAT STUFF

*Colleen Burcar with Gene Taylor*

The
Globe
Pequot
Press

GUILFORD, CONNECTICUT

Cover photos by Colleen Burcar
Text design: Bill Brown
Page layout: Deborah Nicolais
Maps created by XNR Productions Inc.; © The Globe Pequot Press

Photo credits: pp. x, 241, 270: Helen Pasakarnis; p. 35: Dave Ivey; p. 39: Roger Hoffman; p. 42: Greg Slagon; p. 59: Michaud; p. 69: Wayne Bronner; p. 76: Holly Valent, Santa Claus School; p. 90: Larry Lonik, www.morelheaven.com; pp. 94, 139: Travel Michigan; p. 113: David F. Wisse; p. 120: Joe Raymond, *South Bend Tribune;* p. 156: Kathleen T. Lowlor; p. 177: The Leader and the Kalkaskian; p. 199: J. Hoegh; p. 201: Upper Peninsula Travel & Recreation Association; p. 209: Grand Hotel–Mackinac Island, Michigan; p. 222: Loose Data Research LLC at www.JLDR.com; p. 250: Grayling Regional Chamber of Commerce and Grayling Area Visitors Council. All others by Colleen Burcar.

ISBN: 0-7627-0601-5

Manufactured in the United States of America
First Edition/Third Printing

The information listed in this book was confirmed at press time. We recommend, however, that you call establishments to obtain current information before traveling.

# MICHIGAN
## Curiosities

**Help Us Keep This Guide Up to Date**

Every effort has been made by the authors and editors to make this guide as accurate and useful as possible. However, many things can change after a guide is published—establishments close, phone numbers change, facilities come under new management, etc.

We would love to hear from you concerning your experiences with this guide and how you feel it could be improved and kept up to date. While we may not be able to respond to all comments and suggestions, we'll take them to heart and we'll also make certain to share them with the authors. Please send your comments and suggestions to the following address:

The Globe Pequot Press
Reader Response/Editorial Department
P.O. Box 480
Guilford, CT 06437

Or you may e-mail us at:

editorial@globe-pequot.com

Thanks for your input, and happy travels!

To the engaging, big-hearted people featured in this book
who graciously allowed me to label them as
*Michigan Curiosities.*

To my parents, Mary and John Burcar, who, having taught me
the pleasures of traveling both peninsulas of our Great Lakes
State, are now on a heavenly journey of their own as my
newest guardian angels.

# CONTENTS

# ACKNOWLEDGMENTS

I'd first like to thank Cindy Snyder and Mary Sue Brooks of Travel Michigan for getting me started in the right direction on my quest for *Michigan Curiosities*. Thank you to Dianna Stampfler of the West Michigan Tourist Association, a dynamic lady who constantly fed me with food for creative thought. My gratitude also goes out to Shirley Roberts of Bay City; Barb Williams of the Four Flags Area; Carol Potter of Cadillac; Cynthia Asiala of Project Kaleva; Len Trankina of Mackinac Island; Bob Tagatz, Historian and Concierge at The Grand Hotel; Traverse City radio personality Ron Jolly; Shanty Creek's Barry Godwin; Peter Fitzsimons of Petoskey Harbor Springs, Boyne Country; Renee Harlow of Marshall; Dean Woodbeck of Houghton; and the scores of others who helped by providing me with priceless tips about the undiscovered treasures in our state.

Thanks to all my family and friends who didn't see me for months yet continued to provide me with wacky ideas to research, especially Mike Kranson, techno wizard Steve Kranson, Carol and Tom Beeler, Lin Cargo, Donna Joseph, and Annette and Dave Mullet. A special thanks to Lin Celko for giving me the opportunity to write this book and Gene Taylor's wife, Helen Pasakarnis, who gave the project the green light and encouraged me every step of the way.

A heartfelt thanks to my traveling companion, best friend, and husband, Bryan Becker, who drove thousands of miles around Michigan, offering support, insight, understanding, and love. And finally, thanks to Chloe, our 4-pound toy poodle, who, for the sake of quiet curiosity, allowed herself to be smuggled into countless Michigan hotels.

# PREFACE

Allow me to introduce you to Michigan, also known as the Wolverine State, although there hasn't been any sight of the stocky weasel here in decades, and perhaps never was. Rumor has it that during the Toledo war of 1835 (settled without a fight—Ohio got Toledo, we got the Upper Peninsula) an Ohioan got mad and referred to Michigan residents as wolverines, distant cousins of the skunk. The term stuck and went on to become the name of both the official mascot of the University of Michigan and, ironically for many years, the yearbook at rival Michigan State University.

Whatever you want to call me as a 100 percent Michigan homegrown product, I'm proud to be a resident of the nation's twenty-sixth state, the only state in the nation split into two parts. My loyalty to the 96,705 square miles within Michigan's hand-shaped boundaries has never wavered. Born and bred here, I've never had the desire to live anywhere else.

The things that identify me as an authentic local are the same things that make it easy to pick out anybody else from Michigan: I play both pinochle and euchre (although I have a terrible time remembering how to spell either) and can claim at least one friend who's been a queen of some local fruit or vegetable festival. Credit for the latter goes to my buddy Tamara Van Wormer Tazzia who, as Miss Pinconning's Cheese Queen of some years back, went on to become Munger's Potato Queen. To this day, she still savors potatoes, the cheesier the better.

Now that I've verified myself as an honest-to-goodness Michiganian, validating my participation in the writing of a book on oddities in the state, I must tell you that this assignment wasn't, and really isn't, mine. The project originally belonged to Gene Taylor, an incredibly talented man with whom I had the privilege to work for thirteen years.

Frankly, there was no one better than Gene to take on this task, as he himself could be characterized as the quintessential

*Conducting his own "Elvis for President" campaign, Gene Taylor, in a snowy white jumpsuit, was the consummate "good humor man."*

Michigan curiosity. Dressed in his trademark bow tie and ready to work at 5:00 A.M., Gene would spend afternoons cantering through meadows on horseback, followed by evenings serving as master of ceremonies at local charity events. On Wednesdays time after work was filled with service to the Salvation Army, where he'd dish up food to the needy as a regular on the Bed and Bread Truck.

Every wedding needs an Elvis impersonator and, thanks to Gene, mine had the best. His rockin' version of "Blue Suede Shoes" will forever live in my memory as (almost) the most memorable part of the night. No one could keep up with him on the dance floor, as much as we tried. Gene and I once entered a dance contest and, disappointingly, placed second. I'm sure it was my fault we didn't win, since Gene had hip-swinging gyrations that even The King couldn't emulate.

After more than a decade in radio together and several years in television working on *Good Afternoon Detroit* (where he was known as "The Wise Guy"), I was personally grateful for Gene's persistence in bolstering my confidence in my own journalistic skills. If it wasn't for him, I might never have taken a writing position with the *Detroit News*.

Through the years our paths crossed many times—personally, professionally, and even spiritually as members of the Detroit chapter of Christian Media Fellowship. But I was not remotely prepared for the directions our lives would take us next.

In January 2001, with notebook in hand, enthusiastically writing this, his first book, Gene Taylor's life on earth came to an end. News of his untimely passing brought shock and sorrow to the entire Detroit area. His pen and the project had been silenced.

What began as a mournful year continued. Within six months, I faced several unexpected personal losses. Then one night, out of the blue, I was approached by Lin Celko of The Globe Pequot Press. She asked if I'd be interested in completing the *Michigan Curiosities* project. It was obviously divine intervention at work. The book that had been abruptly closed would now be reopened.

Perhaps the manner in which this project fell into my lap could be considered a Michigan curiosity in itself. And so with the blessing of Gene's wife, Helen Pasakarnis, I picked up the pen and finished writing a book that I believe Gene, with his zest for life and unique sense of humor, would have appreciated. I hope you enjoy the results.

—Colleen Burcar

# INTRODUCTION

## BY GENE TAYLOR

**M**ichigan *is* a curiosity or at least full of them. Maybe *contradictions* is a better word but who'd buy a book titled "Michigan Contradictions"? This is a state where we named a car after a president (Lincoln) and a president after a car (Ford). It's the Wolverine State but has no wolverines. Not only can you drive south from Michigan to Canada, if you've got the time, you can drive to Hell (Michigan) and back.

We're the only people in the country who use our hands as a map to point out where we live. On the plus side, we never lose a map and it's a nice change of pace to have people use their entire hand to tell you where to go. And while we call Michigan the Winter Wonderland, we've got more public golf courses than any state in the Union as well as more registered boats than Florida or California.

Michigan is home to the world's largest, most unusual car show. There are incredible dream cars everywhere, but no one will try to sell you a car.

Detroit's Woodward Dream Cruise every August draws tens of thousands of custom cars and more than a million people to stand on Woodward Avenue and watch them drive by. You can see cars with engines so powerful they can pass anything except a gas station. On that summer weekend the clock is turned back to the days of poodle skirts, fuzzy dice hanging from rearview mirrors, and more oil in guys' hair than under their hoods.

Michigan could have been the inspiration for Bambi's mother saying, "Man is in the forest." Every November, hundreds of thousands of deer hunters spend lots of dough and big bucks to try to shoot a doe or get a big buck.

Where else but our mitten-shaped peninsula would you have a city named Novi that has that name to this day because somebody misread a stagecoach map that said the stop was No. VI? (That's number "6" in Roman numerals.)

Canada is north of the United States, but when you drive to Canada from Detroit, you head south to Windsor, Ontario. And as any Detroiter will explain to you, Windsor is really just a suburb of Detroit with different money and stronger beer.

Michiganians eat Coney Island hot dogs that are nothing like hot dogs served on Coney Island, and consume hundreds of thousands of massive Polish jelly doughnuts in a single insane celebration called Paczki Day; waiters in Greek restaurants celebrate their heritage by lighting cheese, a tradition virtually unknown in Greece.

In an election year, pundits will tell you that Michigan is a battleground state. That's because this state is a microcosm of America. When politicians talk about "solid midwestern values," they mean the people here, who work hard and play harder.

Michigan is a collection of the wild and wonderful people, the places they go, and the things they say and do. Over the next few pages, I'd like to introduce you to Michigan Curiosities.

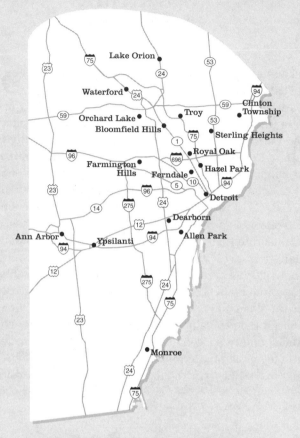

## MOTOWN AND MORE

# MOTOWN AND MORE

**A**lthough Antoine Laumet de la Monthe Cadillac is given credit for founding Detroit in 1701, he was probably just the first to get enough cash from French king Louis XIV to build a fort using the brilliant rationale, "Hey, if we don't do it, the Brits will." So Louis forked over the twelve grand and Cadillac was off to Motown.

*Detroit* is French for "strait," and this crooked strait connected Lake St. Clair and Lake Erie. Antoine would probably be a bit surprised by what most people consider Detroit these days.

According to the *New York Times,* it's the area that swings Michigan and chooses presidents. *Sports Illustrated* has called it the NFL coaching counterpart to the elephant burial ground. Truck drivers first called it *Motown* as an abbreviation for "Motortown," and former auto assembly-line worker Berry Gordy turned it into a fortune. *Rolling Stone* magazine says Detroit audiences are the greatest rock 'n' roll audiences in the world.

But to me, it's a curiosity gold mine.

And it's a pretty sizable gold mine, composed of eight counties and 4.7 million people living in more than 250 separate and distinct municipalities. That's a lot of politicians.

No matter where you look in Detroit, there is something automotive in your face. Visitors coming in from Metro Airport know they're in a "car town" when they're greeted by an 80-foot giant tire that was, in its former life, a Ferris wheel at the 1964 New York World's Fair. The twelve-ton tire has been flat-free sitting along I–94 since 1966.

The thing that makes Detroiters interested in an 80-foot tire is they can just imagine the size of the car it would have to sit under. Detroiter Tim Allen wasn't the first to grunt, "More size, more horsepower!"

That whole "Detroit horsepower" attitude isn't an act with Tim. He's the first one to tell you he's a car guy (the Detroit counterpart to being a good ol' boy down south). To this day Tim loves cars and everything about them. The last time I saw Tim a few years ago, it was at Waterford Hills Race Track just north of Detroit. It was a weekend of historic races. And what was the multimillionaire TV star driving among the classic race cars?

A tricked-out Chevy "Hello-Ralph-Nader" Corvair. That, my friends, is a Big Time Dee-troit car guy.

## *Freeway Royalty Always Tired*
### *Allen Park*

There's one tire out there that surpasses any extended warranty, having seen well beyond 50,000 miles and personally transporting 2 million people around its treads. It's the giant Uniroyal Tire loftily watching over motorists along the I–94 corridor in Allen Park. At eight stories tall and twelve tons, it's grandiose enough to fit any SUV that automakers may be considering in the future.

A shocker for some, the tire came into this world as a Ferris wheel, for the U.S. Rubber pavilion at the 1965 World's Fair in New York. Twenty-four barrel-shaped gondolas carried ninety-six people on each trip circling its circumference, including many of the well heeled. It's been said the Shah of Iran and Jacqueline Kennedy with her two young children, Caroline and John Jr., were among those burning rubber toward the sky.

When the fair closed, the tire emerged as Humpty Dumpty, broken into 188 separate parts for transport to Detroit, requiring four months to be put back together again.

*Detroit's best-known billboard isn't in the city, is
made of rubber, and publicizes a company that
left the state years ago.*

Permanent placement was found as a freeway billboard outside Uniroyal's sales office. A little cosmetic surgery (an
updated hubcap) was performed, followed by work from a color
stylist (neon highlights), and then four years later it got
nailed—literally. As a promotional gimmick for the company's
new NailGard tire, a 10-foot-long, 500-pound nail was ham-
mered into its side.

Uniroyal left town some time ago. The plant was demol-
ished in 1985, but the wheeling wonder remains as a symbol of
strength for today's automotive industry.

Detroit will always be the Motor City . . . so when are we going to see a monster motor?

Designed to withstand hurricane winds, the tire and nail can be seen standing through rain, snow, sleet, or hail, on eastbound I–94, east of Southfield.

## Two Heads Make Beautiful Music Together
### Ann Arbor

**A**h, the sweet roar of an elephant tusk trumpet is music to the ear, at least in India. And in Ann Arbor, where it's a member of the Stearns Collection, the largest assembly of musical instruments in North America.

But these aren't just your run-of-the-mill trumpets or drums. Every piece in the collection of 2,500 is a rare example of how people around the world view the art and science of sound.

Take, for instance, the nineteenth-century "little Tibetan drums"—which, upon closer inspection, reveal their true identity as two skulls tied together like coconuts, covered with animal skins. Shamans believed that the spirit of the person remained tucked inside, waiting to be released by the hands of a capable musician.

Not every piece has the luridness of the cranium twosome or the thighbone trumpet. With greater aesthetic value is the floral porcelain violin from Germany circa 1309 or the taus, a peacock vina from India.

And some of the ideas presented are extremely practical. The Gregorian Chant Book is sized almost larger than life at 4 by 5 feet, so that a single copy sufficed for the whole choir . . . an automatic guarantee that everyone was on the same page.

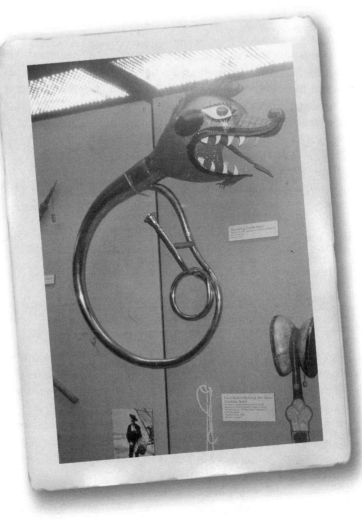

*The sharpest tongue at the University of Michigan sticks out at the music school,*
*firing an arrow from this 1883 dragonhead buzzed lip tromba.*

One section includes a picture of Mary that chanters would kiss, but after accumulating more than a hundred years of saliva, it was decided this wasn't the most becoming page to display.

Most of the instruments were originally in the private collection of Detroit businessman Frederick Stearns as a manifestation of his intellectual interests. Donated in 1899, portions are rotated frequently in the Earl V. Moore School of Music Building, University of Michigan North Campus, 1100 Baits Drive (off Broadway Street). It's open Wednesday through Saturday 10:00 A.M. to 5:00 P.M., Sunday 1:00 to 5:00 P.M. Call (734) 763–4389. Free. Additional instruments will be on display in Hill Auditorium once its renovation project has been completed.

## THE PEAKS AND VALLEYS OF ART
### Ann Arbor

**A**t the university, you're walking along North Campus near the engineering building when you see something curious in the courtyard. At first it appears to be simply lumpy terrain, or some form of crop circles, or a new version of outdoor checkers. But no, it's the Wave Field, an extraordinary earth sculpture by internationally acclaimed artist Maya Lin—creator of the Vietnam Veterans Memorial in Washington, D.C.—made entirely of soil covered with grass.

Commissioned as a memorial to former aerodynamics graduate François-Xavier Bagnoud, Lin was determined to make this piece unique. After an exhaustive study, the decision was made to model it after the three-dimensional wave pattern found on the open sea. Two years in the making, the 90-by-90-foot-square artwork, consisting of grassy waves rising 6 feet from the natural ground, was formally dedicated on October 6, 1995.

Interaction with this monument is not only acceptable, but desirable. Some days you'll see a slew of students with books in

*Forget dusting. It's watering, raking, and weeding that maintain this $250,000 sculpture where students playfully dip into one of fifty grassy waves.*

hand, lying comfortably among the ripples of earth, quietly absorbed in the presence beneath them, perhaps experiencing their personal earthbound version of a Carnival cruise. With that Lin knows that her mission has been accomplished, giving scholars the opportunity to "Explore, study, play, enjoy."

The Wave Field sits in a courtyard adjacent to the François-Xavier Bagnoud Engineering Building at 1320 Beal Avenue. For more information, call (734) 764–3310.

## BLIND AS A BAT . . . NOT!
### Bloomfield Hills

**O**n the one hand, Kim Williams Mies appears to be a fairly typical, fast-paced working mother, devoted to her husband and two children. On the other, she's quite atypical, with responsibilities for the daily care and feeding of nearly a hundred live bats.

When nature called some years ago, she listened and answered. One day at the wildlife center where she was employed as a fresh-out-of-college graduate with a degree in

*Kim Williams Mies whispers to her batty friend to "spread your wings," while those in the background remain hung up on being camera shy.*

zoology, someone brought in what he thought was an injured vampire bat. It was practically love at first bite. Upon completion of her master's research project in "batology," the Organization for Bat Conservation was established, becoming the only venue in Michigan where the furry mammals exist in captivity. (No, they're not birds, although that wasn't scientifically acknowledged until 1920.)

As executive director, Kim's duties are so diverse it would make most people go batty. (I'm sorry, I couldn't resist.) One minute she's stringing swinging chains of watermelon, bananas, and whole heads of lettuce for the daily . . . er, nightly feeding and exercise. The next, it's the placement of frozen pig-bloodsicles, followed by preparation for one of the 1,000 outreach programs delivered annually where inevitably she's sprayed with bat urine.

Martha Stewart, a lover of bats, or depending on your point of view, an old one herself, has given Williams several shots at national TV fame, proclaiming the benefits of these nocturnal wonders. Did you realize a bat with a 3½-inch wingspan can consume 1,000 mosquitoes an hour, or that scientists developed birth control pills with the assistance of female bats? And surprising to most, bats have excellent eyesight. The author of fourteen books on her flying friends, the bat lady has the answer to everything you'd ever want to know and then some.

Milly Hill Mine, in the Upper Peninsula's copper country, hosts the largest colony of hibernating bats in the entire United States—which in some ways resembles the ultimate spa experience. Being the bigger eaters, female bats devour as much food as they can all summer long, achieving a more-than-pleasingly plump figure. Then they enter into their October hibernation period and, almost like clockwork, wake up exactly six months later . . .skinny! Where do I sign up?

In July 2002 the Bat Zone relocated to the site of the former nature center at Cranbrook Institute of Science, 39221 Woodward Avenue. It's open daily mid-June through Labor Day, noon to 5:00 P.M.; weekends only the rest of the year. For more information, call (800) 276–7074 or log onto their Web site at www.batroost.com.

# FOR BEST VIEWING, STAND ON YOUR HEAD

*D*oug West is the antithesis of what he loves to do. A composer, yet he doesn't read a note of music. An author, but he hardly ever finds time to read a book. As a sports artist he's hit a grand-slam home run, even though he's the last person you'd ever tag a "sports junkie."

Painting proved to be Doug's burning passion. At age thirteen, while other kids were out running bases, he'd spend eight or ten hours a day in his basement swinging a brush over canvas. His first subjects were superheroes, but now he exclusively paints sports superstars. It's not about hero worship; the riveting factor was the action and sweeping movements the characters represent.

Personalities like Al Kaline and Steve Yzerman would effortlessly pop out of a color-washed background, until one day the faces all became a big blur. West's world was turned upside down, literally, when the answer for "artist's block" popped out: Turn the figures upside down. What a revelation! No longer Gordie Howe's nose or mouth, they were triangles and ovals (the hockey great's nose surely has been called worse). The furrows on Dick Butkus's forehead became simple lines, without the help of botox.

All facial features reduced to simple geometric shapes, the strokes flowed with more ease, and others took notice. West's work soon found its way into the hands of the president of the Hockey Hall of Fame. Though West was nervous at their first meeting, admitting that his hockey vocabulary was practically nonexistent, his innovative approach and honesty—not to mention his talent—earned him the exclusive title of portrait artist for all three-hundred-plus honored members.

Since then he's gone on to create renderings of five hundred prominent sports figures, including the Great One, Muhammad Ali, who graced his likeness with a personal autograph. Taking one look at West's interpretation, Ali questioned, "Did you paint this?" An affirmative nod, to which Ali responded, "Man, you the greatest." An inverted compliment that Doug will never forget.

To find out more about Doug West's work, it's best to contact him via e-mail at artistdoug@wideopenwest.com or artistdougwest@aol.com. His concept of time is also a bit topsy-turvy—he works until 4:00 A.M., rising at noon.

*Whose famous face is getting Doug West's finishing touch? Hint: A dolphin with a quarter on his back.*

## CAPTURING A BREATHTAKING MOMENT
### Dearborn

The rich and famous give and receive gifts much different from the knickknacks from friends most of us have sitting on shelves. Take, for instance, the largesse of Thomas Edison's son, Charles, who presented to Henry Ford his father's last breath in a test tube. As the famous inventor was passing on, a rack of eight tubes lay next to his bed, and when the final moment arrived, the attending physician was ordered to seal each with paraffin. Sure, it sounds wacky, but you can see for yourself what the not-so-fresh air of Edison looks like in the Henry Ford Museum.

Dubbed "Henry's attic," this world-class collection of memories contains endless hidden treasures to pique an assortment of interests. A handwritten letter dated April 10, 1934, from Clyde Barrow—of the Bonnie and Clyde duo—thanks the automaker for the high quality of the V-8, handpicking the brand as his exclusive getaway car. "For sustained speed and freedom from trouble the Ford has got ever [sic] other car skinned." Expect to hear that endorsement in next year's Super Bowl commercial.

The museum and village together will take you back to another time through actual homes, shops, businesses, and of course Ford's personal gallery of gifts. Don't miss two of the more notorious exhibits: President Lincoln's theater chair the night he was shot and the limousine in which President Kennedy was assassinated.

Touring Henry Ford Museum and Greenfield Village will satisfy every out-of-town guest for hours or days. They're open Monday through Saturday 9:00 A.M. to 5:00 P.M., Sunday noon to 5:00 P.M. Located at 20900 Oakwood, their Web address is www.hfmgv.org. Call (313) 982–6100. Admission is charged; packages are available.

# WILL THE REAL McCOY PLEASE STAND UP?

*A*sk anyone about the Real McCoy and expect to hear answers like, "Wasn't that a television show from the 1960s with Walter Brennan?" or "That was the guy on Family Feud, Hatfields versus the McCoys."

To tell the truth, most people don't realize that there is a single individual associated with the "Real McCoy." Born Elijah McCoy in 1843, he grew up in Ypsilanti to become one of the foremost African-American inventors of all time, awarded the rights to fifty-seven patents. His prized self-regulating lubricator for steam engines became so popular that dozens of oily imitators tried infiltrating the market, prompting wise customers to question, "Is this the real McCoy?"—a phrase born and bred in Michigan that's gone on to become an authentic Webster's entry.

The "Real" McCoy lubricator, patented on March 28, 1882, shares a portion of the Made in America exhibit at the Henry Ford Museum in Dearborn.

### GREEN GIANT SPROUTS WINGS
#### Detroit

A sk anyone in the city, and they'll tell you the Spirit of
Detroit is hockey. To drive home that point, during the
play-offs every year since 1997, the 26-foot bronze *Spirit of
Detroit* sculpture, nicknamed Jolly Green Giant, turns a
brighter shade of red, dressing up in his own Red Wings jersey.

Bob Phillips, vice president of East Side Team Sports in
Warren, is the responsible party, "borrowing" the idea from the
Philadelphia Flyers. He figured, "What the heck," imitation is
the highest form of flattery, let's ease the burden of the *Spirit
of Detroit*, who's been carrying around the weight of the world
for decades, by turning him into the biggest Wings fan this
town has ever seen.

Team captain Steve Yzerman, with his size 50 jersey
(applied to a multiple of 5.5) became the fit model for the 35
yards of cloth, assembled in two days. That was the easy part.

Getting *Spirit* dressed was the nightmare. A metal statue
has a hot temper in the blazing sun, gets a little slippery when
wet, and is about as cooperative as a two-year-old when it comes
to moving a muscle, but when two guys finally were able to
tackle his head and arms they snapped him up just like a pair
of Dr. Dentons. Only to have the shirt erroneously ripped off the
next day by a building supervisor. Another fine example of the
exemplary communication skills in city government.

After all that, the Red Wings did win the Stanley Cup that
year, and the whole process was repeated in 1998, except for
the building supervisor, who was probably transferred to
Philadelphia.

*The* Spirit of Detroit *proudly sports a custom-made,
never-been-washed Red Wings jersey.*

That jersey may be the team's good luck charm—the Red
Wings have been in the play-offs every year since. (It makes
you wonder if *Spirit's* first name wasn't originally Stanley.)

The *Spirit of Detroit,* dressed and undressed, sits on the
west side of the Coleman A. Young municipal building (for-
merly known as The City County Building) at the foot of Woodward and Jefferson.

# FAST FREDDY

*F*ast Freddy is a local boulevardier who makes Beau Brum-
mel look like he shops at the Gap. Featured in a record-
setting six-page spread in September 2000 GQ magazine, his
inimitable style turns heads wherever he goes. Obviously, he's not
too hard to spot; whatever he's wearing, he's sure to be more colorful than a peacock and just as proud. His daily wardrobe
choices are invariably bright: canary yellow, shocking pink, or his
current faves, royal blue and red.

Often referred to as the head-to-toe man, everything he puts
on has to match . . . shoes, socks, pants, shirt, jacket, tie, and hat,
always a hat. "If the outfit doesn't have a hat to it, I don't mess
with it."

Born Fredrick Anderson in 1946, he's always had two jobs to
maintain his passion for fashion. A shoe salesman during his teen
years, it wasn't long before he branched out, becoming a Motown
choreographer, model, DJ, dance instructor (those quick steps
earned him the label "Fast Freddy"), and, for fifteen years, a
nurse's assistant in the operating room at St. John Riverview
Hospital. (No, his uniform wasn't pumpkin orange.)

Remaining consistently a perfect 42 since high school allows
the opportunity for recycling, although Freddy never wears the
same thing twice, at least not in exactly the same manner. Wondering about storage space for 200 pairs of shoes and
countless suits and accessories? Converting the entire
attic of his home into a closet was "the only way I
could survive."

Detroit embraces Fast Freddy, the epitome of
panache, with his powder-blue alligator shoes (he
credits Detroit as starting the reptile foot craze)
and perfectly pressed powder-blue pants. As he
parades around the city, folks of all ages wave
and smile and call him by name.

The latest feather in his cap is working with
senior citizens, teaching them his innovative technique of chair dancing, subtitled "Getting down
while you're sitting around."

You can most likely spot Fast Freddy shopping
at City Slicker Shoes or Henry the Hatter. If he's not
there, they'll know where to find him.

# WHEN THE BRIM HITS YOUR EYES . . . HAT'S AMORE
## *Detroit*

**B**orsalino . . . Dobbs . . . Kangol . . . not a roll call at boot camp. Rather these are some of the head-toppers people have been buying at Henry the Hatter since 1893. Detroit's oldest retail establishment has moved a couple of times to make way for the city's new growth, settling in comfortably at its current location in 1952.

The one and only Henry was Henry Komrofsky. Today it's Paul Wasserman who's carrying on the fourth-generation tradition of fitting the heads of the city's well dressed.

Every Detroit mayor since the doors first opened has walked out carrying a new chapeau in one of the coveted hatboxes.

So how do you make a living from a store filled with nothing but hats, save for the few umbrellas and canes? While you may not see men wearing a formal fedora every day, Wasserman credits his celebrated customers like Kid Rock, Eminem, Barry Sanders, and Lem Barney for keeping the fashion accessory out in the public eye. Okay, so the merchandise appears to be a bit sexist, unofficially labeled "for men only," but women, like Detroit city councilwoman Kay Everett, have been known to break through those barriers and come out looking as chic as anyone.

Obviously business is good. With additional locations in Southfield and Hamtramck, each year 10,000 hats (those with a brim) and 10,000 caps (those with a visor) find a new perch.

Wasserman, who will custom-design anything your head desires, managed to deflate the rumor behind President John F. Kennedy's inauguration. According to his version of the story, a silk top hat had been mailed to Kennedy, which remained unopened until the last minute, when it was then discovered it was too small to wear comfortably the entire day. So sadly for the industry, it was the size of the noggin that gave all future presidents the nod to go hatless their first day in office.

Sizes at Henry the Hatter range from 6¾ to 8, with prices ranging $30 to $300. The Detroit institution is located at 1307 Broadway, open Monday through Saturday 9:00 A.M. to 6:00 P.M. Call (313) 962–0970.

## A Lot to Beef About
### Detroit

It may just be the biggest burger ever made. The owner of Joey's Meatcutters Inn, Joe Gajewski, says, "I've never seen one bigger." Although his restaurant's been around since the 1960s, the thirty-two-ounce gigantic ground round hamburger was added only in the mid-1990s when customers' appetites were expanding, perhaps along with their waistlines.

It's a humongous double-decker . . . two one-pound patties piled high, dressed with lettuce, tomatoes, onions, and pickles. Add on five and a half ounces of cheese and you've got a real gut-buster. It stands so tall, it arrives at your table with a steak knife stabbed through the middle just to hold it together.

You may be wondering, Does anyone finish one of these monsters all by himself? Absolutely. Gajewski says he sells at least twenty-five every week to people of all shapes and sizes who polish them off single-handedly.

What makes them so satisfying is not only their size, but also the fact that the meat is the freshest you'll find anywhere. The eatery is located in the heart of Eastern Market, and the sixty to eighty pounds of beef served every day is never frozen; it's ground daily right next door. Even the buns are specially made a few blocks away at the Milano Bakery.

*The ultimate odd couple: Joey's 32-ounce burger, with an estimated 12,845 calories (give or take a few), and a zero-calorie Diet Coke.*

On the menu you'll find mini versions at half a pound for $3.25 and a one-pounder for $4.75. The colossal portion will set you back $8.25.

And the government apparently has given its stamp of approval to the big burgers . . . One afternoon, filling three separate tables, were agents from the IRS, FDA, and FBI.

Joey's Meatcutters Inn is located at 2638 Orleans. Hours are Monday through Friday 9:00 A.M. to 8:00 P.M., Saturday 10:00 A.M. to 4:00 P.M. Call (313) 393–0960.

# TUBE STEAK ON A BUN ARIA

**W**hat do opera and mustard have in common? Charlie Marcuse. Although most Detroit Tigers fans might not know his name, they recognize him instantly when you refer to him as the "Singing Hot Dog Man."

First employed as a vendor in 1998 when he was sixteen, he quickly developed his inimitable style of hawking, with an operatic voice that could clear the back fences quicker than some of the hits on the field.

He's mindful of why the crowd is there, and never croons during the home team's time at bat. Admittedly, he says, while kids love his shtick, some adults have found his rare method of peddling a bit annoying. There's no question he's the consummate cheerleader; he's been known to get half the ballpark singing "Happy Birthday" to an unsuspecting fan.

Speaking of springing a surprise, Marcuse has even been a facilitator in a couple of successful marriage proposals, popping the questions musically in between hot dog sales.

His produce line is limited to one solo item by his own choosing, because, he says, "A hot dog is the only authentic baseball food." And don't ask him for anything but mustard or he'll quickly catch you up on a little trivia. For years, he claims, only mustard was offered at ballparks because sugar-laden ketchup was a bee magnet.

You can catch Charlie at any of the roughly eighty home games at Comerica Park at 2100 Woodward Avenue in Detroit, right behind home plate on the third-base side. For ticket info, call (248) 25–TIGER.

# BEWARE THE TWO-HEADED BOOKWORM
## *Detroit*

This place should come with a warning: Bibliophiles may find the contents habit forming. With more than a million titles, John K. King Used and Rare Books has been satisfying the public's hunger for the printed word since 1965. Once inside the main building, you can easily lose yourself for hours combing through 30,000 square feet of shelves and shelves of books on every topic imaginable. It's all highly organized, and the staff is extremely helpful if you should be in need of direction.

A book about founder and owner John King could easily fill volumes. Defining himself as "the legendary two-headed bookworm," he was bitten by the literary bug in high school. He found his way into the business world shortly afterward. In 1983 he purchased his own building, which has quite a history itself. Originally the Advance Glove Factory Building, rumors have been around that one day in 1949, the employee-filled edifice was literally picked up and moved to make room for the impending freeway! King swears it's true, adding he has the confirming photographs locked safely away.

King has become a master at instantly recognizing the value of any tome. Using his "sixth sense" and a relatively simple equation, based on supply and demand, he personally assesses each item. Recently baby boomers have driven up the price of Dick and Jane readers, which were never allowed outside the classroom. Thanks to the nostalgia trend, the primers are selling now for anywhere between $40 and $100.

Some of the more valuable "finds" are next door in the former Otis Elevator Building. Larger than its neighbor at 50,000 square feet, the rare-book room has a museum-like quality,

hosting myriad signed, first-edition pieces from the likes of
Babe Ruth and John F. Kennedy. It's here that you'll also find
the collection's oldest printed book: a Bible from 1491.

Prices of all works range from "free" (you'll always find a
box of gratis goodies sitting at the front door) to "up to the
stratosphere."

John K. King Used and Rare Books is located at 901 West
Lafayette Boulevard in downtown Detroit. Hours are 9:30 A.M.
to 5:30 P.M. Monday through Saturday. Call (313) 961–0622.

## PAST AND PRESENT DANCIN' IN THE STREETS
### Detroit

As a kid, Jerome Meriweather lived across the street from
2648 West Grand Boulevard and watched inquisitively as
three teenage girls and a middle-age woman would get in and
out of a limo for hours, without ever going anywhere. Later he
came to appreciate the girls as the Supremes and the woman as
Maxine Powell, their etiquette coach, teaching them how in
ladylike fashion to enter and exit the vehicle in a mini skirt.

RESIDENT GRIOT—a tribal historian—is the title on Jerome's
cap nowadays as he stands inside the famous address on
Hitsville, USA, home to the Motown Museum. If the walls could
talk, they'd resonate with the same stories he's sharing about
the music industry phenomenon of the 1960s, founded by
Berry Gordy Jr. with an $800 loan.

This stucco two-story studio where Gordy resided was in
operation twenty-four hours a day, seven days a week turning
out hit after hit from young Detroiters like Smokey Robinson,
Stevie Wonder, and Diana Ross, who all did double duty as

record packers and rest room cleaners.

Everything inside is open for the public's perusal, left exactly the way it was, with flooring worn out by dancing feet and piano keyboards marked with stickers for artists who couldn't read music. Polish and pizzazz show up in the representative costumes . . . Michael Jackson's black fedora and white sequined (right hand only) glove and the Supremes' splashy sequined gowns, each weighing in at an astounding thirty-two pounds. No wonder they were all so thin—you couldn't help but lose weight carrying that extra baggage.

There's even an opportunity to try out your voice in the famed echo chamber, guaranteed to make anyone sound good. Don't get your hopes up for a recording contract, though. Motown headed to California in 1972, and was eventually sold for $61 million. Even though Gordy still maintains a home on Boston Boulevard, he's not around to put your record to the lunch test . . . where he'd ask random citizens if they'd prefer to spend their money on the music or a sandwich. If the song got one sandwich vote, it was never released.

Definitely worth a trip to "Stop in the Name of Love" of Motown memories, the Motown Historical Museum is open Sunday and Monday noon to 5:00 P.M., Tuesday through Saturday 10:00 A.M. to 5:00 P.M. Tours leave every hour. The address hasn't changed—2648 West Grand Boulevard; (313) 875-2264. Admission charge.

## NO REFUSE REFUSED
### Detroit

A trip down Heidelberg Street is like entering the Disney World of recyclables. Tires, shoes, vacuum cleaners, street signs, broken dolls, cardboard taxis . . . all strewn across lawns

*The city calls it junk; the owner calls it art. The mouse atop the*
*OJ House (obstruction of justice) concludes it's a toss up.*

or hanging from trees. Houses, adorned with so much old junk you can't make out the windows from the doors. Despite all this, there's a sense of whimsy that appears to have artistically awakened an otherwise tired neighborhood.

That was the objective of artist Tyree Guyton when he created the Heidelberg Project in 1986, only to be met with acrimonious assaults from local politicians, claiming it wasn't art at all, but just an unorganized heap of trash. Five years later city officials sprang a surprise attack, bulldozing four of Guyton's bedazzled homes.

Perseverance paid off, and today the project stands as garish as ever. For a picturesque pick-me-up, polka dots permeate almost everything paintable. Inspired by his grandfather's love of jelly beans, Guyton started out painting the dots on houses, then trees, then the pavement, "and I wish I could polka dot all the people, too."

In cooperation with a local elementary school, Guyton educates young people in his style of "street art," pleased to see that the block he grew up on is stamped, hopefully for a long time to come, with his personal trademark.

Plans next are to strip one of the vacant homes and, with the aid of Liquid Nails, cover the sides, roof, porch, all of it with pennies. Now *that* sounds like a house that would make sense to anyone.

The Heidelberg Project gets more than 275,000 visitors a year. It's located on Heidelberg Street on Detroit's East Side between Elery and McDougall; a detailed map is accessible through their Web site: www.heidelberg.org. For other inquiries, call (313) 537–8037.

## A FEATHER YOU CAN BOWL OVER
### Detroit

**H**ere's a solution for the sports fan who has trouble deciding whether to spend a few hours involved in a tantalizing game of shuffleboard, bocce ball, or horseshoes. Try feather bowling, a unique fusion of all three, that arrived in Detroit with Belgian immigrants during Prohibition. It takes the worry out of breaking a nail on traditional bowling balls.

The playing field is a 70-foot concave trough, or alley, covered with an appealing mixture of dirt and ox blood. (Not as gross as it sounds, bearing a close resemblance to tightly packed sawdust.) Each participant takes a three-and-a-quarter-pound wooden ball having an imagined similitude to dinosaur

*In almost one hundred years the only thing that's changed on these bowling lanes is the feather.*

dung and whirls it down, watching it traverse the lane on its way to the upright feather waiting at either end. Closest to the tickler scores a point. Ten points and your team claims victory.

The Cadieux Café is the only place in the country where feather bowlers can hang out. Not a thing has changed on the pair of lanes that have been here since 1929, not even the faithful league members who show up every night during the week for a game of three-on-three. Participants say, "Drinking doesn't hurt the camaraderie either."

The Belgian influence extends to the beer—described as "funky"—and the food. Well known for its mussels, once a Friday-only item, Cadieux currently makes them available daily, although connoisseurs say for the best flavor, eat them only in months containing the letter *r*.

A pleasurable party activity, feather bowling lanes are available for rent—$25 an hour weekdays, $40 weekends. Cadieux Café has occupied the corner at 4300 Cadieux for almost a hundred years. It's open every day 11:30 A.M. until 2:00 A.M., except Sunday when it doesn't open until noon. Call (313) 882–8560.

In 2000 Bath City Bistro in Mount Clemens opened three feather bowling lanes, but they're covered with a compressed rubber padding. The health department said no to the plasma–dirt and food combo . . . Cadieux Café's age kept it grandfathered. The Bistro—which has had its plumage pushed around by Pamela Anderson and Kid Rock—rents lanes by the hour also. Find it at 75 Macomb Place, (586) 469–0917.

## *A  WOOD-BURNING  STOVE  MADE  OF  WOOD?*
### *Detroit*

For years people wondered, "What's the deal with the giant stove?" Well, unbeknownst to many, Detroit was once known as the Stove Capital of the World. At least five major companies here were producing wood-, coal-, or coke-burning stoves in the late 1800s. Today a classic reminder of the town that was really cookin' sits high above busy Woodward Avenue.

Dubbed the "World's Largest Stove," built for the Michigan Stove Company's exhibit at the 1893 World's Columbian Exposition in Chicago, it's 30 feet long, 20 feet wide, and stands approximately three stories tall at 25 feet. It's made entirely of wood, all Michigan oak, even though most people think it's metal. A unique paint job provides the metallic appearance.

The gargantuan stove has been somewhat peripatetic.

*Construction of the world's largest stove ignites curiosity.*
*It's made entirely of Michigan trees.*

Initially after the Expo, it sat in front of the stove company on
Jefferson Avenue, near Elmwood and Adair. In 1927 it stayed
on Jefferson, but moved just west of the Belle Isle Bridge. And
in 1965 it was moved to the Michigan State Fairgrounds, a
trek of about a dozen miles. So as not to disturb traffic, the
midnight move on a flatbed truck was done discreetly—as discreetly as can be done with a fifteen-ton stove.

The weather took its toll on the manufacturing icon, and in
1974 it was taken down, piece by piece, and placed in storage
at the Fort Wayne Museum. There it lingered for more than
twenty years until John Hertel, general manager of the Michigan State Fair, decided to fuel new life into the aging monolith.

After countless hours of restoration, the treasured landmark was ready to reveal her face-lift to the world on August 24, 1998. The elderly stove has returned to her old state fair stomping grounds at 8 Mile and Woodward. And she looks better than ever, although it would have been so much easier if she had been self-cleaning.

The best viewing is from Woodward, just north of 7½ Mile Road. For more information, or to purchase a memorial brick, contact The Stove Project, Michigan State Fair Exposition Center, 1120 West State Fair, Detroit, Michigan 48203, or call (313) 369–8254.

## WOODWARD DREAM CRUISE
### Detroit Area

*D*etroiters still refer to themselves as East Siders and West Siders, with Woodward Avenue as the dividing line. Compared to these allegiances Jerusalem is one big happy family.

Every August, however, the same street that divides Detroiters also brings them together for an event called the Woodward Dream Cruise. It's the world's longest, largest, and loudest free automotive event, with more than 30,000 custom cars, hot rods, muscle cars, and antiques cruising up and down Woodward Avenue through eight cities. Add the music, food, and crowds, and it "ain't nothin' but a party."

Where else but Detroit would 2.5 million people line a street to watch cars drive by? Charles Brady King would probably roll over in his grave. He reportedly drove the first automobile down Woodward in 1896. But the inspiration for the Woodward Dream Cruise has a more recent history.

In the 1950s, the eight-lane road tempted young men fueled by cheap gas and testosterone poisoning to bring their wheels to Woodward to do a little cruising. There was no better way to impress the bouffant-haired, poodle-skirted ladies at drive-in restaurants like Ted's and The Totem Pole. The hottest of the hot rods competed on Woodward in an attempt to become king of the road. Legend has it that the Big Three tested their top-secret project cars many a night after dark on Woodward.

The godfather of the Woodward Dream Cruise was Nelson House, a man looking for a way to raise funds for a kids' soccer field. He and a group of volunteers launched the nostalgic Woodward Dream Cruise. What was supposed to be a onetime event became an annual trip in a time machine. Although technically the Cruise takes place on the third Saturday in August, car enthusiasts bring out their chariots to get in the mood for an entire week.

The thirty local charities in the seven host cities of Berkley, Birmingham, Ferndale, Huntington Woods, Pleasant Ridge, Pontiac, and Royal Oak all benefit from the sale of official merchandise and refreshments sold at the Woodward Dream Cruise. The cruise generates $55 million in economic impact for Oakland County, but more importantly, it gives middle-age men the chance to remember the two things they miss from their youth: horsepower and hair. For information, call (888) 4–WDC–1963 or visit www.woodwarddreamcruise.com.

# THE POLISH MUSLIMS

There aren't many bands that would begin the PR blurb on the back of their CD with, "A few short decades ago, the Polish Muslims were only known to patrons of after hours rave parties and penitentiary inmates."

But the Polish Muslims aren't just any band. If Lawrence Welk and Tina Turner had a child and it was adopted by Sly and the Family Stone and Monty Python, you still wouldn't have all of the nuances they put into their music. As Dave Uhalick puts it, "Our music is just, well, it's none of your business what our music is."

The eight-member band is a mainstay in the Detroit area, playing gigs for anybody who wants an instant party with their "polka 'n' roll." Although the idea of a polka beat dropped in periodically along with an accordion solo in the middle of a rock classic like "Dance to the Music" may take some getting used to, fans of the band have done just that. Their concerts are a cross between a mosh pit and a Polish wedding.

The lyrics to their songs rest strongly on their Detroit roots and include so many references to the area that you need a Detroit dictionary to translate. Their second CD—titled, appropriately enough, The Polish Muslims Make #2—features a cover festooned with more local photographs than a chamber of commerce brochure. Song titles like "Where Hamtramck Is" (sung to the tune of "Where the Action Is") and "Paczki Day" (to the tune of "Yesterday") mean very little to anyone who doesn't know that Hamtramck is a working-class Polish enclave and a paczki (pronounced poonch-key) is a jelly doughnut, served the Tuesday before Ash Wednesday, with the density of a paperweight.

The surprising thing is the band is becoming much more than a local phenomenon, drawing crowds all across the Midwest at places that wouldn't know a paczki from a pizza. Their name alone has made them a favorite at Polish festivals, although they make a point of explaining the group isn't your typical polka band. They're more your typical "Rock 'n' Roll Out the Barrel" polka band.

And when it comes to competition . . . What competition?

You can e-mail the Polish Muslims at thepolishmuslims@aol.com.

## Mr. Unordinary
### Farmington Hills

As I approach the entrance to Marvin's Marvelous Mechanical Museum, the 9-foot clock overhead says I'm two hours late for my appointment. How could that be? A second glance provides the answer: The timepiece is running backward, with all numbers and hands going counterclockwise, a tip-off to the antics inside.

Showers of neon splash everywhere, and among several busloads of keyed-up kids, I spot owner Marvin Yagoda, who's playing hooky from his day job. A full-time pharmacist, his animatronics apparatus "museum" is the result of "a hobby that got out of hand." It's filled with a hodgepodge of coin-operated machines—no count on how many, but all 1,000 electrical outlets are in full use—from a 1923 motorized fortune-teller to a series of high-tech video WaveRunners.

Marvin is the Willy Wonka of electromechanical gizmos. At one point he gathers a crowd to watch Marvallo the Buffalo lose his temper, when billows of smoke spew from the animal's nostrils. Next, a young lady is beckoned over to the counter where a sign cautions DANGER OF HIGH WINDS. Riotous laughs break out as a breeze blows up her legs.

With fifty airplanes circling the ceiling in conveyor-belt fashion, I can barely hear when Marvin tells me he's quenching the public's thirst for anything involving love and torture. Passing by the "Love Pilot"—which, for a quarter, promises to "steer you straight" (a much different meaning in the 1920s)—to instead pay 50 cents to watch an electrocution, it soon becomes apparent that agonizing pain is the hands-down favorite.

*Pharmacist Marvin Yagoda's vintage carousel administers a dose
of good medicine to happy kids.*

I choose to drop my last coin on the "Most Disgusting Spec-
tacle" as a handful of anxious third-graders stand by starry-
eyed. The mannequin resting inside begins to move one hand,
prompting us to all shriek a nauseated "ooh," followed by a
chorus of outrageously silly giggles. I walk away confident my
money was well spent.

Marvin's Marvelous Mechanical Museum is the right pre-
scription for fun at any age. Located in the back of a strip mall
at 31085 Orchard Lake Road, it's open seven days a week. Call
(248) 626–5020 or log onto www.marvin3m.com. Free to get in,
but load up on quarters. Refreshments available.

# DAVE IVEY

*D*avid Greg Ivey is a very strange man. But then again, most artists are. What makes Dave really unusual is that he enjoys being called "unusual." Most artists don't wear their art and have it judged in bars. That happens every Halloween when Dave hits the Halloween costume circuit dressed as everything from the Volcano God to a saxophone-playing rhinoceros.

Dave is a foam sculptor, and his art involves turning pieces of foam into just about anything you can imagine . . . and some things only he can imagine.

You don't really have to understand art to enjoy Dave's work. A smile will do nicely, thank you very much. Dave began making people smile when he first worked as the art director on the infamous Ghoul Comedy Show *out of Cleveland that was on from 1971–1975 on channel 61. The program was kind of a cross between a one-man* Saturday Night Live *and* The Munsters.

In 1978 Dave read an interview with Jim Henson, who was asked how the Muppets were made. Henson revealed that they were sculpted out of foam rubber and covered with terry cloth. That was all Dave had to hear. He had a foam-rubber mattress in his basement, and with his trusty electric turkey carving knife, he went to work making a Godzilla costume for his two-year-old son.

By the time the mattress-to-monster metamorphosis was complete, Dave knew he had found his calling. Dave creates one-of-a-kind costumes that would make the bar scene in Star Wars look like an accountants' convention. He explains, "When you see a monster-type costume in a movie that moves various body parts, there are probably four or five people or computers making it move by remote control. At a costume party, everything in my costumes has to be done by the person inside."

To say that Dave's costumes "move" doesn't give you the entire picture. "In all of my costumes," he notes, "I'm able to drink through the finger. I call it the Mork finger." That doesn't count the fan within the costume for cooling purposes. In fact, most of Dave's artwork has more gimmicks than your typical luxury car. Although both may blow smoke, Dave does it intentionally.

When Dave's wife first complained her monster costumes weren't feminine enough, Dave placed smoke-blowing skulls in the

Dave Ivey performs eye-popping stomach surgery
on his foamy friend.

appropriate places. The skulls are not only less expensive and safer than implants, but they attract more attention as well. If they attract too much attention, she simply activates the strobe light in her cleavage to encourage her admirers to "lighten up." I guess she wants her costumes to be loved for more than just a great set of skulls. Dave has a few tricks for his own costume, too. Not only does his latest creation have glowing eyes, but the eyebrows can be raised for that added touch of cynicism.

What began as a hobby has turned into a profitable venture for Dave, who's in demand by companies looking for one-of-a-kind promotions for events or conventions. Even though Dave compares the costumes to a self-contained astronaut suit, he does admit there is one major difference: answering Mother Nature's call. When asked how he can go to a five-hour party without a pit stop, he shrugs and says, "You just deal with it." And I imagine you keep your Mork finger out of drinks. Dave Ivey can be reached at (248) 894–3985 or you can e-mail him at krakatoa@juno.com.

### WATCH THE THUNDERBIRDIE
### Hazel Park

**E**very year at Christmastime the friendly folks at Neiman-Marcus put together dream items for their catalog. In the 2000 catalog one hot seller was the new two-seater version of the Ford Thunderbird. In twenty minutes they sold off their entire consignment of 200 of the new T-Birds at $41,995 a copy. Plus tax, title, et cetera, et cetera, et cetera.

That kind of excitement is great news for Bill Gill and his crew at the Thunderbird Center in Hazel Park, Michigan. Bill, who already ordered two of the new Birds, thinks that the interest in the new car is going to make the original even more valuable. That's good news when you sell parts to make classic T-Birds like new.

The Thunderbird Center only sells parts for 1955–1957 Thunderbirds. And although Bill no longer restores the cars himself, his knowledge of the so-called Baby Birds is legendary. Bill used to teach judges what to look for in competition.

Although many of the orders they fill are for items like a horn ring for a '57 or an automatic shift-selector chrome knob, you could build an entire car from scratch from the parts here. Buying each part individually would make it about a $500,000 vehicle, but it could be done.

It's tough to figure out exactly how many Baby Birds are still around these days, but the Thunderbird Center sends out more than 14,000 catalogs every year and fills in excess of 6,000 orders.

Eric Dennett, who fills most of these orders, routinely ships parts to Spain, Portugal, Denmark, Sweden, Australia, Grand Cayman, and Japan, where American cars from the 1950s are hugely popular.

But the foreign order that sticks out in Eric's mind the most is the one he sent to Germany. "I got a call from a customer who wanted a fender for a '57 Thunderbird shipped to him overnight." Eric jokingly said the only way the shipper could do it was to cut it in half. That was fine with the Bird Man of Germany, so Eric cut the $3,000 fender in half, charged the $700 shipping, and three days later got a call saying the fender was on the car, painted and ready to roll. Unfortunately, Eric didn't have parts for the vintage Mustang the man's girlfriend had just wrecked.

The Thunderbird Center is located at 23610 John R. Road, Hazel Park, Michigan 48030.

Call (248) 548–1721 or visit www.thunderbirdcenter.com.

## DRAGGIN' LAKE ORION FOR MONSTERS

*T*here are a million reasons behind the acquisition of high school mascots. Practicality bred the Dearborn Fordson Tractors, named for the nearby Ford tractor plant. In Bad Axe, it seems logical the Hatchets take the field. But there's quite a story behind the Lake Orion High School Dragons.

*It all started back in 1894 when several ladies, on a leisurely cruise in their rowboat, reported spotting a real dragon vaulting its ugly head out of the water. The town was horrified, and for several years the account kept everyone on shore.*

*With numerous sightings, the frightful tale steadily grew. The monster once was believed to have been at least 80 feet long, devouring everything in its path including cows that had gone astray.*

*Alas, there was a happy ending to the yarn when the elusive creature was identified as a set of rims from wagon wheel pulleys that a young lad had covered with canvas and anchored in the lake. With the truthful discovery, the suggestion was made that the ladies of Lake Orion in the future restrict their drinking to well water.*

# CUSTER STILL STANDS

**P**eople in Monroe refer to Steve Alexander as the "guy who portrays General Custer." Spend some time talking to him and you'll walk away convinced there's a stronger power seeded within.

First, there's the striking natural resemblance to the famous general. While he's on the job as a surveyor, strangers habitually stop and ask, "Did anyone ever tell you that you look exactly like General Custer?" Okay, so the physical similarity could be a fluke.

Steve was also an accomplished reader at an extremely early age. Before long "General Custer's thoughts had found a place inside a three-year-old boy." Obsessed with his hero throughout his school years, his book report topics never strayed. A check on his personal library shelves today reveals more than 1,000 books on George Armstrong Custer. All happenstance?

A stop at Montana's Big Horn Museum in 1986 to go to the bathroom, the fulfillment of a lifelong dream (not the bathroom part), proved to be a critical turning point. Dressed in his customary cowboy boots and a buckskin jacket purchased at a garage sale, Steve fell into the path of Diana Scheidt, organizer of the Big Horn reenactment, who claimed she had been searching for "the man who knows more about Custer than Custer knew about himself." No training required, he immediately fell into uniform, diffusing Custer's persona. Merely being in the right place at the right time?

Contrary to signs along I–75, Monroe is not the general's hometown; his birthplace was New Rumple, Ohio, which has taken Steve under its wing, naming him the city's official General Custer. Lectures across the country, movie and television appearances, including Unsolved Mysteries, searching for the accurate story of the general's death (theories say he was humiliatingly smothered by a 300-pound woman), and a string of reenactments keep Steve away from home forty-eight weekends a year. Or at least they did until he got busy restoring the house he recently purchased—the very home George and Libby Custer lived in together during the 1800s.

Maybe it's all just a coincidence. Maybe not. Either way, Steve Alexander never complains about "becoming my childhood dream."

You can contact Steve by e-mail at TheGeneral@georgecuster.com, or check out his Web site www.georgecuster.com.

*Mirror images. Is that General George Custer or Monroe's Steve Alexander?*

## M A K E   M I N E   M A R S H   R A B B I T
### M o n r o e

The focus of this highly coveted culinary experience isn't a meal from Emeril, but rather an opportunity to experience a 200-year-old cultural tradition of savoring the wintertime delicacy commonly known as . . . muskrat. Each January and February dozens of churches, VFW halls, and private clubs in Monroe host bountiful banquets with the little furry rodent as the main event. (The fur is gone; a number of small bones remain.) Credit goes to the French settlers, who were so fervent in their taste for muskrat that they requested and received special dispensation from the church to allow its consumption on Fridays.

A strict vegetarian, the marsh rabbit—as they call it here—has been reported to be one of the cleanest animals around, if not the cheapest. At last check the critters, any size you want, were going for a buck apiece.

So don't knock it till you've tried it, and those who have say an incomparably sweet, buttery flavor has even the biggest skeptics coming back for seconds. Of course, it's all in the preparation. Localites favor the rich "so-dark-it's-almost-black" meat parboiled in wine with carrots and onions, topped with a creamed corn gravy.

If you can't get into one of the "club" dinners, try Ernie's Gathering Place, which for half a century has been satisfying daring dietary demands with its wild game feasts, starring none other than Monroe's beloved 'rat. In the background you can almost hear the Captain and Tenille crooning a melancholy chorus of "Muskrat Love."

Ernie's Gathering Place, where Great Lakes snapping turtle is always on the menu, can be found at 1525 South Dixie Highway, Monroe; (734) 242–2330. For word on other muskrat munchings, call the Monroe Historical Society at (734) 240–7780.

### SKELETON CREW PERFORMS SEASONAL YARD WORK
#### *Orchard Lake*

**P**icture this: A guy is digging up his front lawn, installing plastic sumps the size of overgrown barrels everywhere, all because he says he wants to relive those happy childhood memories of Halloween. Wouldn't buying a case of Milk Duds be a lot easier?

Greg Slagon is so "obsessed and possessed" with the pagan holiday that for the past decade, he's transformed his entire yard into a cemetery every Halloween. Mind you, not a real one, although people have stopped to ask how his house could be built around so many grave sites. Greg's is instead a series of whimsical tombstones, talking skeletons (popping out from the buried sumps), and Dracula thrusting out of a coffin.

Awestruck by the Haunted House at Disney World (deprived as a child, he didn't make his first trip there until he was twenty-five), he signed up for animatronics classes—and the rest, as they say, is history.

Each October his home is shrouded in special effects: billows of smoke, thunder, lightning, squeaking gates, life-sized rubber bats with blinking eyes, a beating heart, a flickering candelabrum. Cars jam the narrow street, and luckily, the neighbors don't seem to mind the commotion. Some have even loaned space in their trees to accommodate the overflow of Bela Lugosi mannequins.

Every year the show is revamped. It runs ten to twenty minutes and then resets itself from a garage-based control panel, resembling in size and shape the main switchboard for Ameritech.

It's hauntingly bizarre, but then Greg is no ordinary hellion, and Roseanne, his wife of twenty-five years, is supportive. "I just close my eyes."

*With "budding" monster heads and skeletons, fall planting takes on new meaning in the front yard of Greg Slagon's home.*

People always want to know two things—Why? "Because I never had toys with batteries." And how much does this extravaganza cost? "A lot of money plus 20 percent."

According to Greg, the "Wards Point Cemetery" (named for his residential street) will go on indefinitely, as long as "I don't run off to the Caribbean, get committed, or have my wallet taken away by my family." It's generally ready to go the first week in October. Specifics can be obtained by calling (800) WE–BURY–U or visiting www.wardspointcemetery.com. Admission is free, although a coffer gratefully accepts donations for local police and fire departments.

## Mark Ridley—King of the Castle
### Royal Oak

Just about all the comics you've ever seen on a late-night talk show have horror stories about the time they spent "on the road." Comedians are the wandering minstrels of the MTV age, and they accept it as a chance to pay their dues and hone their craft.

Comedy club owners have heard it all, but Mark Ridley has an empathy that few other owners can match: Mark's entire club has been "on the road" ever since he opened it in January 1979.

His first "Comedy Castle" was part of a restaurant northwest of Detroit called the Meeting Place. The first night, nine local comics played to a full house of ninety people. Mark booked comics with potential "and big families to assure a crowd." A young Tim Allen cut his comedic teeth there.

Mark stayed there until fall, when he expanded to a strip mall down the street to the 200 seats of Friday's Old World Café. He was there just over a year—long enough for comics to become familiar with the location—before it was time to hit the road again.

He moved the business farther down the same street to a placed called Stafford's, and then to a club called Maxmillion's.

By this time Mark and his traveling circus of comics were giving performers a source for material. The standard line of "Anybody here from out of town?" was hardly appropriate, since the audience could stay put and Mark would be the one from out of town.

Comic Dave Coulier, who played Joey on ABC's *Full House*, got his start playing Mark's various Comedy Castles and said the running gag was that Mark changed locations so often, he should have given the acts frequent driver miles. Most of

Mark's clubs, like Laffery's, were downstairs from popular restaurants. The joke was that Mark spent more time in basements than a shop vac.

Mark tried a combination restaurant–comedy club centrally located on Woodward Avenue, the area's main drag, but eventually decided he wanted people to laugh at his acts, not his food. Mark's alumnus wall is a Who's Who of the comedy world. At one time or another he's had Jay Leno, Jim Carrey, Gary Shandling, Robert Wuhl, Jerry Seinfeld, Dennis Miller, Jeff Foxworthy, Paul Reiser, and Detroit native and film director Mike Binder, who was then working as a comic. Mike went back out to L.A. and told his fellow comics that there was a good comedy club in the Detroit area playing with checks that didn't bounce even if the club did bounce around.

Mark Ridley's Comedy Castle location du jour is in Royal Oak, where Mark remodeled the old Royal Oak Tribune offices and printing plant to turn it into a 400-seat showplace. The Castle's been there for a while, so hopefully Mark will no longer live by the slogan "Have Mike, Will Travel."

Mark Ridley's Comedy Castle is found at 269 East Fourth Street. Contact (248) 542–9900 or www.comedycastle.com.

### GLOBE-TROTTING JET-SETTERS: THIS SPUD'S FOR YOU
#### Sterling Heights

Imagine being photographed on the Great Wall of China, returning to the United States, hopping a plane for a photo shoot with a holy man in India, coming home for a day, flying to Turkey for a wedding, making a quick exchange at the airport, and it's off again for a fiesta in Mexico City. Sound exhausting? Not to the Sterling Heights resident who's been living this hectic itinerary since 1998 with no signs of slowing down. His world may seem rather plastic . . . which is an accurate assessment since this nomad is a 2½-inch Mr. Potato Head.

The traveling tuber is the brainchild of Judy Bobchick, property manager of Cambridge Apartments, attractive to international businesspeople because of its short-term leases. When one of her tenants asked to have his mail taken in for three months while he worked in Africa, Bobchick agreed if, in return, the Hasbro toy she had found in the courtyard an hour earlier could go along. A few weeks later pictures of Mr. Potato Head on his wildlife safari were posted in the mail room, and soon residents were clamoring to accompany him to more than fourteen countries and a jaunt in the Caribbean for some island-hopping. Demand for his companionship grew to such an extent that when a flight delay in England threatened his departure to the Philippines, an "understudy" was found at 1:00 A.M. in an all-night store to save his tour guides from disappointment.

Packing is no problem—he travels light with his own disposable camera—although one couple found it necessary to buy their own underwater camera so Spudman could join them on a scuba diving expedition.

Don't worry, loneliness isn't a concern on the holidays. Cambridge House owner Rick Rosenhaus gave the mustachioed monsieur a Christmas present never to be forgotten: a personal photograph taken on December 24 at the Wailing Wall in Jerusalem.

With three cases filled with memorabilia now on display, residents eagerly await chronicles of each new adventure. On the upcoming agenda: Australia, Lebanon, and finally a long-awaited twelve-state tour of the USA. Not a bad way to celebrate Mr. Potato Head's fiftieth birthday . . . but the golden boy would like to know what the airlines are doing with all his frequent flier miles.

Cambridge House is on 16½ Mile Road. Reach Judy there at (586) 264–0690.

## OUTHOUSE WHIZ KID FAIRLY FLUSHED
### *Troy*

**Y**ou've got to ask yourself, Why in the world would anyone want to become an expert on outhouses? For the answer you'll have to go to the John in charge of the Outhouses of America Tour, John Loose of Troy. In the early 1990s, his sister began giving him a miniature outhouse every year to remind him of a funny experience he'd had with a raccoon in an outhouse as a child. That gave him the idea to start the "tour," to literally preserve a vanishing piece of history that almost every home had in the past. Now in his forties, he's been photographing and collecting freestanding potties from all over the country for more than a decade.

Deciding to share his love of the loo with the rest of the world, he developed an exhaustive Web site jam-packed with everything from his incredible photography collection to toilet trivia. Do you know why most outhouses contain two holes to sit on or why there's a quarter-moon found above the door on most of them?

It's a virtual tour of some of America's most historical outhouses. It's had close to half a million visitors, with many of them so enthusiastic they contact Loose to have their own houses put on the journey.

And of course, at the end of the tour there's an on-line boutique, where you can purchase books such as *Hidden Assets—Stories Behind the Throne* and other goodies ranging from outhouse jewelry to a hand-painted toilet seat.

John Loose thinks it's kind of nuts how popular the tour has become. He says he's not really proud of his extraordinary knowledge, but admits he's gaining a worldwide reputation. He's even been contacted by England's Thomas Crapper & Co.

Ltd. for assistance in displaying reproductions of the original flush toilet.

Take the Outhouse of America Tour at www.jldr.com. Contact John Loose at Loose Data Research LLC, 2240 West Square Lake Road, Troy, Michigan 48098-5225; the fax number is (248) 813–0384.

## IT's NOT EASY BEING GREEN

*T*he thought of millions of worms crawling around at their workplace would probably make most people shudder. But for the employees of DMF Bait Company, it's a sign that business is good. The more creepy crawlers there are, the better they like it.

The first larva leeched on in 1977, and ever since the number of creatures entering the building has risen dramatically; now the company can boast of 119 million Canadian nightcrawlers passing through their doors. That makes them the largest wholesale bait distributor in the world. Worm searching at Wal-Mart? You'll find them . . . the chain is their No. 1 customer.

And not all worms leave looking the same way as they came in: 2.1 million undergo a makeover that leaves them green. Not just any green, but a kryptonite-looking green. Chris Fry, inventory manager, says they get more repeat customers for their green worms than anything else. Apparently some people think the green ones give off an odor that the fish find exceptionally attractive. What's in the green dye that causes fish to bite? Fry's lips are sealed, saying, "It's a trade secret."

DMF is strictly a wholesale operation, but know that when you hook up the next wiggler, he's most likely been here in Waterford.

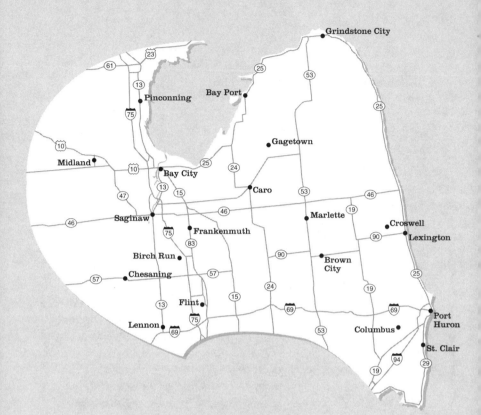

## THUMB AND SOME

# THUMB AND SOME

**W**hen someone gives a "thumbs up," it's the universal sign for "A-OK," "That's it," "You done good." The region included in Michigan's thumb certainly exemplifies all of those . . . giving an outward sign of approval of our state for the rest of the world to see.

We'd like to share a thumbnail sketch of our far east, where countryside meets 150 miles of lakeshore. It's a top-producing area for dry beans (Michigan is second in the nation), corn, and sugar beets (Michigan is fifth in the United States in sweetness from the ground, first in sweetness of disposition of its population). Bound by Lake Huron, here you can hold vigil for the numerous fish—salmon are among the best thumb suckers—and international freighters as they pass up and down the St. Lawrence Seaway.

The thumb is one of three Michigan points connecting to a foreign country with the opening of the Blue Water Bridge in 1938, linking Port Huron to Sarnia, Canada.

And now some rules of thumb:

- Wear comfortable shoes
  - To promenade the longest freshwater boardwalk in America in St. Clair.
  - To walk on the natural breakwall in Grindstone City, made of broken grindstones, or the 4,750-pound Grindstone Memorial at the corner of Copeland and Rouse.
  - To climb the ninety-four steps of Michigan's oldest lighthouse at Fort Gratiot in Port Huron.
- Keep your head up and eyes open when traveling through Marlette and Brown City, both known for UFO sightings.
- Head to Bay Port, the village where the fish caught the man, at least once in your life the first weekend in August for Bay Port Fish Sandwich Days to sample their secret-recipe two-fisted fish sandwich.
- Keep an open mind as you thumb through the other curiosities of this section.

## GHOSTS, LEGENDS, AND TABLE 14
### Bay City

**G**host sightings are so plentiful in Bay City, Casper should become the area's official mascot. Tales of debauchery gush out of historical publications. But a fix is close at hand for the hordes of inquiring minds who want to know more about the wicked ways that once existed here. New in 2002, the "Ghost, Legends, and Lore" tour begins smack dab in the middle of "Hell's Half Mile" (once filled with 147 saloons) and doesn't stop until you've been through a dozen of the city's most popular haunts.

Michiganians love their Paul Bunyan. The fabled lumberjack is believed to have been modeled after Joe Fournier, whose ghost has been roaming the upper halls of The Campbell House since the time of his murder there in 1875.

Simmons Jewelers feels the presence of Orville, a worker who years ago refused to be fired. One female employee was convinced of Orville's ghostly spirit when he left a dusty handprint on her behind.

The granddaddy of them all is Old City Hall, with two jail cells in the basement and two phantoms casting a "creepy aura" on the restaurant inside. First thing every morning, manager Rose Grappin heads over to examine Table 14. She swears the bits of coal she finds are the ghost's nightly deposit.

The Ghosts, Legends, and Other Bay City Lore Trolley Tour runs through the Bay County Historical Museum for an exclusive group of twenty-eight every Saturday at 2:00 P.M. Advance tickets are recommended; call (989) 893–5733.

Old City Hall Restaurant, 501 Saginaw Street, is open Monday through Thursday 11:00 A.M. to 10:00 P.M., Friday and Saturday until 2:00 A.M. Closed Sunday. Call ahead for Table 14: (989) 892–4140.

# TWO STRIKES, MADONNA'S OUT

*I*n the buff caused the rebuff of Madonna in the town where she first crawled out of the womb. The key to the place was made, polished, and ready to be handed over in 1985, but the mayor of Bay City said No Way, José, or words to that effect. He was not about to let Madonna, whose nude body had just been found disgracing the pages of Playboy and Penthouse, unlock one tiny iota of his community.

Then two years later the "Material Girl" let her feelings be known to the world during an interview with Jane Pauley on the Today show, describing her birthplace as "a smelly little town in northern Michigan." That did it. Get out the tar and feathers. And definitely take back that Italian sculptor's 13-foot statue. Officials unanimously agreed that Bay City was not an appropriate place for the artwork. Everyone was in shock. Madonna appeared so happy as a little girl visiting her maternal grandmother's home on Smith Street. Why would she say such a thing now?

An apology and explanation came the next week during her concert at the Pontiac Silverdome: "I didn't mean the people of Bay City stink, just the Dow Chemical Plant." Yeah, right, easy to say to people who just spent three weeks' pay to get in to see her.

The rumor mill works overtime in Bay City with claims of "Madonna" sightings on the streets of downtown, occasionally passing by the home that still exists on Smith Street, or at the cemetery in Kawkawlin where her mother is buried. Word is she ties a scarf around her head, wears dark sunglasses, and is still looking for that key.

## HEAD OVER HEELS IN LOVE
### Bay City

When Bay City schoolteacher Anna Edson Taylor fell for a man, she fell so hard . . . well, hard enough to go right to the front page of the record books as the first person to successfully barrel over Niagara Falls. Allowing herself to be strapped into a cushion-lined barrel made expressly to her specifications by the West Bay City Cooperage Company, Anna was going to find fame, fortune, and a trip to the altar with her fifty-year-old lover.

On October 24, 1901, her sixty-third birthday (although she'd led everyone, even her boyfriend, to believe she was forty-three), the barrel was given a heave-ho for a raucous seventeen-minute ride down the rapids of the Horseshoe Falls. Upon retrieving it, the few observers present were shocked to find her alive, without a single broken bone, and able to convey clearly her profound words of wisdom: "No one ought ever do that again."

Sadly, there were no offers for athletic endorsements, no book deals. Nor did any proposals for marriage materialize. Taylor died twenty years later, brokenhearted, penniless, and buried in a pauper's grave in Niagara Falls, New York.

More than fifty years went by before the Bay City Chamber of Commerce committed to changing the status of this daredevil's unrecognizable name by bringing her body home for a more dignified burial. Any feisty old broad who subtracts twenty years from her age, and gets away with it, indubitably deserves better.

But two sides butted heads in court: the city and the Annie Taylor Preservation Society, who fought desperately to keep her remains in New York. After months of legal haggling, it was learned that Annie had left no lineage to approve the transfer, forcing the issue out of the halls of justice.

An Annie Edson Taylor memorial in Bay City's Veterans Memorial Park has been bantered about, but no final approval has yet been stamped on the proposed waterfall sculpture.

This high-spirited Bay Cityan who was the first to conquer the falls was followed by eight men and another woman. At least 150 have lost their lives trying to barrel, kayak, or JetSki over. Anyone caught making an attempt today will be given jail time and a $25,000 fine on the American side, $10,000 in Canada.

## TONY'S: HOME OF MONSTROUS MEALS
### Birch Run

No calorie counters are allowed at Tony's I–75 in Birch Run, where a typical breakfast consists of three eggs, three slices of toast, a whole pound of bacon, and another whole pound of hash browns. All that food will lighten your wallet by only $6.25, although if you decide you want to share and need an extra plate, that's another 50 cents.

Don't think the big meals with the small prices are going to end anytime soon. The Lagalo family has been running Tony's for almost fifty years, and there's no sign of slowing down. On an average weekend they'll serve more than 1,500 hungry customers, who will consume about 1,000 pounds of hash browns and 600 pounds of onions.

The pace is quick, and the 200-seat dining room is almost always full. In fact, it's rare that you won't find a line waiting to get in. With the crowds stretching out to the back of the building, Tammy Johnson, daytime manager, says sometimes it seems "like people are hatching out in the parking lot."

Everything on the menu is served oversized and *portion control* is not in anyone's vocabulary. After a hearty lunch or dinner, be sure to save room for their most popular item—the banana split. They start with a whole banana and then pour toppings over more than half a gallon of ice cream!

The waitstaff is sassy and the cooks are geniuses. There are no computers and no handwritten tickets. An order is simply yelled out; in a matter of minutes, it's ready for delivery.

On your way out, if there's an empty corner in your tummy, you can pick up some free candy—about thirty cases are given away each Saturday and Sunday. When your experience is over, you'll likely walk away humming Tony's theme song, sung to the tune of "Jingle Bells":

> *Tony's Grill, Tony's Grill, that's where we all go*
> *When we want to get fed up right from head to toe.*
> *Tony's Grill, Tony's Grill is the place we pick*
> *'Cuz we know, while we're there, we'll eat so much, we're sick.*

Tony's I–75 in Birch Run (exit 136) on 8781 Main Street. Call (989) 624–5860. It's open Sunday through Thursday 7:00 A.M. to 9:00 P.M., Friday and Saturday 6:00 A.M. to 11:00 P.M.

## THE PLACE TO "BE . . .WITCHED"
### Caro

The minute you pull up to the solid black building with two large gargoyles peering down, you know something inside is different. Anonka's Witch Museum opened in the small rural community of Caro on January 5, 1999, and it's been a bewitching experience ever since. Founder Anonka is neither a witch nor a psychic, but claims she's "a sensitive" who can read others through tarot cards and crystal balls.

A progression of chambers covering 9,000 square feet leads you through a gallery of the supernatural. A menacing entrance in the Mystery Room aims at conquering your fears. Enter the murky tunnel and a surprising world of enchantment awaits you at the end: a cosmos with fairies and flowers and the sounds of calming waters.

Only in this palace of the paranormal would you find an entire room devoted to bowls that sing. Not just any bowls, but quartz bowls that play a tune of healing energy as you stand under a pyramid with a crystal hanging over your head like mistletoe. The downstairs dungeon resembles a haunted Halloween display with ghoulish ghosts and goblins and a blood-dripping fountain.

If all this witchery has whet your appetite for weirdness, stop by Pharaoh's Phudge Room for some chocolate-covered ants. Or venture over to the Witch Way Café for some "eye of newt" served in flaming cauldrons.

The obligatory gift shop is in the front, enticing you from the minute you open the door to buy some floating-eyeball or bleeding-finger candles.

It's all in good fun and not intended to scare anyone, at least not too much. Anonka's creativity and energy appear to be endless, but then by her own admission she knew she was "abnormal" since she was nine months old. By age seven she named herself Anonka. Anonka? That's right . . . no last name, "just like Cher."

Anonka's Witch Museum is located at 119 North State Street. The hours are Sunday, Wednesday, and Thursday 10:00 A.M. to 5:00 P.M., Friday and Saturday until 7:00 P.M.; closed Monday and Tuesday. Call (989) 673-7747. Admission to the museum is free. There is a small fee to tour the dungeon.

# OHOWIH8OHIOST8

**T**he rivalry between alumni of Michigan State University and the University of Michigan has never been a laughing matter for die-hard fans. Either you bleed green or you're true blue through and through, and you'll do almost anything to prove your devotion.

In the 1970s, as chairman of the Michigan State Highway Department, U of M grad Peter Fletcher was taking a lot of heat for granting permission to have the Mackinac Bridge repainted green and white. What? His colleagues were appalled to learn that the team colors of the chairman's archrival would now be boldly displayed on the world's longest suspension bridge. How could such a thing be allowed to happen?

Turning a few shades of red, Fletcher decided to surreptitiously put his own stamp of loyalty into his work. While working on a new state highway map to commemorate the opening of Detroit's Renaissance Center, he persuaded a somewhat nervous cartographer, who shall remain nameless, to give birth to a few new cities that only Wolverine fans could appreciate. When the 1978 official state map was introduced, within the Ohio border were two clandestine towns named Goblu and Beatosu. So what? Nothing was done to falsify the Michigan map. Everything within state lines remained totally accurate.

More than a million copies were distributed, although most today appear to be missing in action. One of the few remaining recently was auctioned off for $1,200.

If by chance you spot an official Michigan highway map lying around from 1978 with a picture of the towers of the Renaissance Center on the cover, look closely near Bono, Ohio, just east of Toledo. Find the fictitious Goblu on it and you've got one of the originals, likely worth a lot of money.

A cautionary note: You can't judge a map by its cover. Be sure to carefully check out the insides. There are before-Fletcher and after-Fletcher versions, the latter sans the bogus Buckeye listings.

Decades later Fletcher, now president of the Credit Bureau of Ypsilanti, still gets teased about the episode, which only strengthens the pride in his Wolverine smile.

## DAM THAT RIVER . . . IT'S SHOWBOAT TIME!
### *Chesaning*

O n the sides of buildings, the water tower, the welcome sign
. . . everywhere it screams at you, the same words: CHESAN-
ING, THE SHOWBOAT CITY. There's no question, there's no business
like showboat business here. This village of 2,500 could easily
teach Madison Avenue a thing or two about hyping a product.

"Here comes the Showboat! This means at least as much to
this village as the World Series does to any city in the nation—
probably more." Chester Howell, editor of the local weekly
newspaper, shared those sentiments in 1950, thirteen years
after his friendly persuasion mellowed the naysayers enough
to launch the floating stage.

The *Shiawassee Queen*, a 120-foot replica of a paddle
wheeler, has become a permanent fixture, every year hosting a
hundred local cast members who sing and dance their hearts
out as they cruise down the river, heading toward the dock fac-
ing the 6,600-seat amphitheater. All just a warm-up act for
Marie Osmond, the Smothers Brothers, or some other equally
famous bigwig.

The volunteer dedication has made this splashy event what
it is today. Thousands of hours of behind-the-scenes work,
stringing lights, sewing costumes, rehearsing, coordinating
schedules, selling tickets, all for a showboat that runs only six
days a year. Seems a shame it's so short. But it couldn't be any
other way . . . the shallow Shiawassee River requires damming
just to get the boat to float.

The *Queen* makes only two encore appearances, once as a
backdrop for graduation, the other at Christmas, getting all
decked out in holiday finery. The rest of the year it's moored on
M57 by the bridge.

Reservations for showboat tickets are accepted starting in
mid-April. To place an order or for info year-round, call (800)
255–3055.

# WALK UP AND TOUCH THE STARS

*M*ove over, Graumann's Chinese Theatre. Step aside, Planet Hollywood. Make room for the Chesaning Showboat Star Walk.

Bobby Vinton, in 1991, was the first to bend over and place his hands in wet concrete, leaving his permanent impression for all to admire. Each year after that the Chesaning showboat's headliners have been asked to repeat the process with their personal branding. There are now thirty-four Hollywood squares lining the pavement in front of the chamber of commerce office. They're not easy to spot from a distance and up close may even be mistaken for a set of gravestones, inscribed with the year of the star's appearance.

Don't let that scare you. Lots of people step forward to size up the palms. Anxious to see how I measured up to the big names, I tried my hand against Kenny Rogers . . . too big. Brenda Lee . . . too small. Frankie Valli . . . just right. Franki Valli? I wanted to . . . but then I remembered, "Big Girls Don't Cry."

The Showboat Star Walk is right in front of the Chesaning Chamber of Commerce at 218 North Front Street. Call (800) 255–3055.

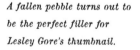

*A fallen pebble turns out to be the perfect filler for Lesley Gore's thumbnail.*

# WORLD'S LARGEST TEDDY BEAR
## Chesaning

**T**eddy bear collecting isn't just for kids anymore. Currently it's the fourth largest hobby for adults in America, but for nearly thirty years it's been No. 1 in the hearts and wallets of Terry and Doris Michaud, makers of the Guinness-authenticated world's largest teddy bear.

Created in 1988 for a special exhibit at Disney World, Yankee Doodle Teddy measures 24 feet from his butt to the peak of his stars-and-stripes top hat. Picture a belt size 240.

Teddy was all stitched up and ready to go when—like the sailor who builds a boat in his basement—the Michauds discovered they needed a way to get their plush creation to Orlando. Where do you find transportation for a bear with arms 11 feet long? You don't. So you

*Terry Michaud, along with his wife, Doris, and Bill and Rosemary Hayes, put in 5,000 man and woman hours to create this 1,930-pound cuddly curiosity.*

build your own carrier and pray that it doesn't rain. Failing to waterproof Teddy's Styrofoam core was the one oversight that could have instantly created a two-ton King Kong.

The next year, one of those offers-you-can't-refuse came in and today the stuffed patriot sits at an undisclosed location while the Michauds are back in Michigan tending to their smaller-scale bear business, writing books and lecturing on their favorite topic.

Terry takes it as a compliment when friends tease that he's entering his second childhood, retorting, "I don't think I ever left my first."

Carrousel Teddy Bears and Antiques charms customers seven days a week in the summer, 10:00 A.M. to 5:00 P.M. It's located at 505 West Broad Street. Call ahead for fall and winter hours: (989) 845–7881. Do-it-yourself bear kits are available and ready for assembly, in almost any size.

## FILL 'ER UP, NEIGHBOR!
### Columbus

When Debbie and Jay Olah purchased their 1871 farm-house, part of the deal was their inheritance of a tired old chicken coop sitting in the backyard. They were faced with the same question as many homeowners—what do you do with something you don't have any use for, yet historically still has value? Creatively speaking, the Olahs laid a golden egg. Down came the wire, up went the walls. Voilà! A 1930s gas station.

A sensible solution for the family whose dining room was already brimming over with their fascination for collecting vintage gas pumps. So more than a dozen pumps left the main house for the outhouse, where some stand guard around the

*"What a gas!" That's the reaction to the unusual lawn
ornaments in Debbie and Jay Olah's backyard.*

exterior and others are tucked neatly inside. But the hobby just
wouldn't quit. "The Coop," as it is affectionately called, now
holds hundreds of never-been-opened oil cans, racks of original
Shell travel maps, a cigarette machine, a jukebox, and almost
anything else you could ever think of related to filling stations.
It's used primarily as a place to party; they've even re-created a
bar inside where you can step up and get a little personal
pump-up.

In an effort to maintain the functioning appearance of the
station and "because it's kind of a kick," the lights on the
pumps are set on timers, and every day at dusk the colorful
neon signs radiate throughout the neighborhood. Jokingly,
those close by have said it's so bright at night, they fear the

whole town will have a brownout. Seriously, though, Jay says the community enjoys it, especially the electric company.

The Olahs' main house hasn't been forgotten, with its own distinct personality. With the couple's incessant love of antiques trading, an ivy-covered, kewpie-doll kitchen was the recipient of an exchange of an old Coca-Cola canoe for a 1928 General Electric refrigerator. Their stove is a 1925 original, and despite their mileage, both appliances are in perfect working order.

While everyone in town knows the house with the gas station in the backyard, you can find it north of 34 Mile Road, 4 miles west of Gratiot, at the end of Bauman Road. For directions, information, or to offer a trade of any gas-related items, call Jay or Debbie at Halo (that's Olah spelled backward) Floor Covering at (586) 727–3459.

## CONNECTOR TO THE
## MOTHER-IN-LAW . . . SWEET
### Croswell

**O**ozing with sugary sweetness from every corner—that's been the reputation of the city of Croswell for more than a century. The arrival of the Michigan Sugar Company inaugurated it all when it began lusciously converting more than 300 tons of sugar beets into a reported 44,668,730 pounds of taste-satisfying crystals every year.

At the turn of the twentieth century, all the hardworking townsfolk loved to enjoy their free time at River Bend Park on the west side of the Black River. It wasn't easy to reach, though: They were forced to hike a long, roundabout path available only from the south. Good Samaritans, in the summer of 1905 city officials raised $300 to build a footbridge across the river, spanning 139 feet.

Shortly after it was erected, David Wise, a major proponent of the project, put up an overhead sign on the west end declaring BE GOOD TO YOUR MOTHER-IN-LAW. No one's exactly sure why those words were chosen, although theories run rampant. Some say couples contemplating marriage would often walk hand-in-hand over the bridge. What better way to keep those hands together for eternity than with a little in-law coaching? Others say everyone knows to be nice to your mother, but a friendly reminder may be needed to ensure that kindness to a

*A bridge to mend troubled waters when the in-laws become out-laws.*

mother-in-law. Or possibly it's a retort to Ernest Wild's observation, "However much you dislike your mother-in-law you must not set fire to her."

Constructed of 455 wooden slats and standing 25 feet above water at its highest point, it shakes and creaks and rattles and rolls as you saunter across. Even the slightest external force (perhaps a nudge from an in-law?) may find you quickly engulfed in not-so-hot water.

Michigan's only suspension footbridge can be accessed by turning off Howard Avenue, the town's main thoroughfare, onto Maple. The renamed Swinging Bridge Park is right at the end. For more information, call (819) 679–2299 or visit www.croswell-mich.com.

## *PUFF AWAY: AN ANSWER FOR EVERY PIPE DREAM*
### *Flint*

**M**ichigan is the only state in the Union that *doesn't* grow tobacco but *does* have a government proclamation for Pipe Smoker's Week. That's thanks to the efforts of Paul T. Spaniola, the world's foremost pipe authority and owner of Paul's Pipe Shop in downtown Flint since July 12, 1928. That's not a typo—Paul was just fifteen years old when he opened his doors for business. His shelves now stock a million different smoking devices, one as artfully crafted as the next, running the gamut from wooden cowboy boots and eighteen-carat gold umbrellas to a $2.69 corncob pipe.

Always smoking, or "supposed to be," as founder of Paul's Institute of Pipe Smoking, he taught Susan Hayward how to become a feminine puffer for her role opposite Charlton Heston in the 1952 movie *The President's Lady*.

*Paul Spaniola has snuffed out the competition to earn the*
*designation of the world's greatest pipe smoker.*

Six-time world pipe-smoking champion, (whoever can keep
3.3 grams of tobacco going the longest without relighting
wins), Paul's personal collection, housed in the second-floor
museum, includes the pipes of all the world champions since
1949. Also on display is his "trophy," the 1897 pipe of mega
millionaire C. S. Mott, with whom he shared many a good
smoke throughout Mott's seventy-five years of lighting up.

Paul holds dear the visitors from all over the world who
stop in to say hi, catch one of his famous card tricks, or buy a
pipe or two. As a sign of appreciation, for years he reciprocated
by sending out birthday cards to every person who ever bought
a pipe, a practice he abandoned after the post office changed its
forwarding policy.

Born on January 29, 1913, this father of twelve (ten girls and two boys fighting for the bathroom), grandfather of fifty-one, and great-grandfather of eighty-three comes into work every day to whip up one of his 200 secret blends of tobacco, with fragrant whiffs of cherry vanilla, Georgia peach, chocolate, or Louisiana coffee grabbing you the minute you open the door.

Forget about all those highfalutin political theories. Hope for world harmony may lie in one tobacco-filled tube. As the gospel according to Paul says, "If everybody smoked there would be no wars." Pass the peace pipe, please.

The Arrowhead Pipe Smoker's Club meets the first and third Tuesday of each month at Paul's Pipe Shop and Pipe Hospital (all brands of wounded pipes cheerfully healed) located at 647 South Saginaw Street. It's open Monday through Friday 9:00 A.M. to 7:00 P.M., Saturday until 5:00 P.M. Paul's there when the day begins, but usually heads home by late afternoon. Reach him at (810) 235–0581

## *WHY DID THE CHICKEN CROSS THE ROAD?** *
### *Frankenmuth*

Frankenmuth, Michigan, could be the model for towns that want to reinvent themselves.

In the 1950s when the I–75 expressway bypassed M–83, the city's main street, Frankenmuth had to react. The city fathers knew their town—which had become known to salesmen, hunters, fishermen, and tourists as a stop on their trip up north—needed an attraction. It was sister city Gunzenhausen,

* To get out of Frankenmuth.

Germany, that realized the answer: the city's Germanic roots.
They guessed right, and now Frankenmuth is one of the top
tourist attractions in the state, drawing more than 3 million
visitors annually.

According to Annette Rummel, the CEO of the Frankenmuth Chamber of Commerce, the city's name comes from the
Bavarian province of Franken; *muth* is German for "courage."

Courage was something the earliest missionaries had when
they left their homes in Germany to come to the area to teach
the Native Americans the ways of Christianity. Others from the
same area followed, and before long the town was a Bavarian
community, complete with the language and customs of their
homeland. A big part of that heritage was the hospitality that
necessitated hotels and restaurants in the city. Zehnder's of
Frankenmuth is ranked the eighth largest restaurant in the
nation based on total sales. Along with the Frankenmuth
Bavarian Inn Restaurant, the town's landmark restaurants are
known for "Frankenmuth-style" chicken dinners. Zehnder's
alone serves approximately a million guests per year, who consume 840,000 pounds of chicken, 628,000 pounds of cabbage,
110,000 pounds of vegetables, and 26,000 pounds of coffee. The
third generation of Zehnders still serve family-style. The heap-
ing platters of food would be enough to make even Elvis
"Return to Zehnder's."

Still, as good as the food is, it takes more than a hearty
meal to attract more than 2,000 motorcoach group tours annually. The city offers year-round activities beginning in winter
with an international snow- and ice-carving contest. In May the
World Expo of Beer takes over, with 150 types of brew from
around the world available. The June Bavarian Festival
includes parades, arts and crafts shows, and (naturally) traditional German food.

Then on the Fourth of July you can try to get rid of all
those calories in "Volkslaufe" or "People's Race," which draws
more than 2,000 runners or roughly the same number found
in line for a Sunday chicken dinner at Zehnder's.

The list of events never ends, but on the remote chance that the week you visit isn't part of a "something-fest" you can visit the wood-carvers, sausage makers, clock shops, winery, Glockenspiel Tower, and a partridge in a pear tree . . . down the road at Bronner's CHRISTmas Wonderland.

Frankenmuth is east off I–75 between Flint and Saginaw. For information, call (800) FUN–TOWN—that's (800) 386–8696.

## *Bronner's CHRISTmas Wonderland*
### *Frankenmuth*

With all the talk about the commercialization of Christmas, you'd think the world's largest Christmas store would be front and center to begin holiday decorating just after the Fourth of July. But before you even get inside the seven and a quarter acres or five and a half football fields of Bronner's complex, that preconception disappears. For one thing, there's the spelling. Everywhere you look at Bronner's, the name of the store is written CHRISTmas Wonderland. That's not an accident. Nor is the Silent Night Memorial Chapel.

With special permission from the Oberndorf, Austria, city government, Bronner's erected a replica of that city's Silent Night Memorial Chapel. That original was built on the site of the St. Nicholas Church where "Silent Night" was first sung in 1818. The 56-foot-tall chapel was built in tribute to the famous Christmas hymn, and in thankfulness to God.

That same theme permeates everything you hear from founder Wally Bronner. At the beginning of the video about the store that is shown in the theater, the perpetually red-jacketed seventy-five-year-old Bronner tells audiences the motto of the store is "Enjoy CHRISTmas, It's HIS Birthday; Enjoy Life, It's HIS Way."

*At a height of 17 feet, this bigger-than-life Santa is one of three that's been greeting customers at Bronner's for more than thirty years.*

Wally has the energy level of a nine-year-old on a post-Halloween sugar rush as he runs around the store greeting some of the better than 2 million visitors who pass through his doors every year. In fact, during the single weekend after Thanksgiving, over 50,000 shoppers check out everything from Nativity scenes to mistletoe with 6,000-plus styles of decorations, including MERRY CHRISTMAS greeting ornaments in more than 70 languages.

In his copious free time, Bronner gives more than 250 speeches per year. He says he has the luxury to do that now because the day-to-day running of the company has been taken over by, as Wally says, "Our second generation serving your second generation."

Wally and his wife and partner, Irene, have come a long way since 1945 when everything got started, and for people who have a long way to come, Wally shows them how to get to the shop. He has more than seventy billboards around the country, including the one on I–75 near Ocala, Florida, just north of Disney World.

Bronner's CHRISTmas Wonderland is found at 25 Christmas Lane, P.O. Box 176, Frankenmuth, Michigan 48734. Call (989) 652–9931 or, for recorded information, (800) ALL–YEAR. The Web site is www.bronners.com. Bronner's is open 361 days a year.

## *Fixin' Your Bird*
### *Frankenmuth*

**E**ver wonder where to go if your cuckoo won't "cooke"? The Frankenmuth Clock Company has heard it all. Head cuckoo corrector Carol Wilcox says that since the clocks are mechanical, the biggest problems are caused by a lack of maintenance. The clocks should be cleaned and oiled every few years. And indeed, customers come here from all over the Midwest to get their birds oiled by Carol and Company and see the 800 clocks in the store.

Cuckoo clock aficionados will tell you that there are two types of birds: musical and nonmusical. You also have a choice of a one-day clock or the seven-day variety, both of which are wound by pulling up a traditionally pinecone-shaped weight on a chain that gradually travels down and moves the inner workings of the clock. That chain is probably why the cuckoo wristwatch was never a big seller.

Cuckoo clocks date back to 1760 in the Black Forest of Germany. One of the local clockmakers got tired of the same old chime sound that was commonly used and replaced the bell tone with the cuckoo bird native to the area. The body of the cuckoo clock we know today is made to resemble a railway stationhouse, which evolved after the railroad came to the Black Forest.

The original clocks were made completely of wood, and many of today's clocks are still hand-carved. They range in size from small wall versions to a grandfather cuckoo clock made by the Dold Company in Germany. The 6½-foot clock is hand-carved out of basswood and includes a seventy-three-note Swiss music box that plays two different tunes. The carvings include two horses, a water fountain, a little boy, and a little Bavarian forest. If Bill Gates were a cuckoo, this clock is where he would live.

The choices of clocks vary from the simple single-bird model to versions that include dancers coming out of various doors of the railroad station spinning to a variety of musical tunes.

Imagine the Radio City Music Hall Rockettes and the Village People in lederhosen. In fact, I think one of the Village People did wear lederhosen.

Don't be disappointed if the hour passes and all the cuckoo clocks in the shop don't sound off. The birds are all safe in their houses until someone asks for a demonstration.

I personally would like a cuckoo that sounded like a flute, but even the Frankenmuth Clock Company doesn't have one flute over the cuckoo's nest. The store is located at 966 South Main; (989) 652–2933. Open seven days a week, 9:00 A.M. to 6:30 P.M.

### EIGHT SIDES ARE BETTER THAN FOUR
#### Gagetown

It's Michigan's largest eight-sided barn and it sits practically in the middle of nowhere. Driving up to it, you'd think you were in Kansas, where the roads are flat surrounded by farmland.

That's the case in Gagetown, where the thumb's Octagon Barn garners attention from admirers across the country. Part of the 520-acre Mud Lake Estate, it was constructed in 1923 by the president of the Gagetown State Savings Bank, James Purdy.

It's unlike any barn built at that time in Michigan. First, it's tall, standing about four stories high at 70 feet. The octagon is formed by eight outside walls, each 42½ feet high, creating 8,600 square feet of space. A 29-foot loft provides another 6,200 square feet of elevated storage space. In short, there's plenty of room for any animal . . . Noah's entire Ark would have fit without a problem.

When you step inside, you feel as if you're in the middle of an old western movie. You hear creaks and squeaks from the constant breeze that filters throughout, and it's easy to envision farmers pitching mega barrels of hay. The barn is filled with farming memorabilia, like the 1908 New Deere Cylinder Hayloader.

Officially the Octagon Barn is open only for special activities. Tours usually occur in August, followed by Fall Family Days in September.

While the gate outside the property is locked, the barn itself most often is not. So you're free to walk about at your leisure. The Friends of the Thumb Octagon just ask that you sign the guest book and turn the lights out when you leave. Contact them at P.O. Box 145, Gagetown, Michigan 48735; (989) 665–0081; www.thumboctagonbarn.com.

The barn can be found, though not easily, 1½ miles east of Gagetown on Richie Road, north of Bay City Forestville Road in Tuscola County. Signs point the way.

## LAWN ORNAMENT CAPITAL
## OF THE WORLD
### *Lennon*

**S**omewhere, someone is losing sleep right now worried over how he's ever going to find the ideal adornment to spice up his boring lawn. Rest assured, Michigan has the concrete solution.

Acres of cement figurines shaped like gargoyles, sombreros, turtles, and anything else that's ever appeared in your worst nightmare fill the outside of Krupp's Novelty Shop.

It's the brainchild of Jean Krupp, who in 1950 was so poor she started selling wooden doghouses made out of trashed orange crates on her front lawn. Acting on a suggestion to include the sale of concrete birdbaths, her assortment expanded and so did her profits.

More than half a century later, on the same front yard

where it all started, rows and rows of indescribable "stuff" are organized with a hint of madness to their method. Signage over Row 5B introduces angels, fire hydrants, and fruit baskets. Farther down, it's an aisle of jockeys and Dutch couples.

Customer buying habits change. For a while their biggest sellers were "bend-over butts," but that trend has fallen through the cracks. Now it's anything that spews water, except maybe their re-creation of Michaelangelo's *David*, which was found by a shopper to be anatomically incorrect in its proportions.

Inside, the store hosts collectibles and things not so collectible . . . like that decoupaged plaque of Elvis.

Is there anything too tacky to sell? Employees say they've almost given up on finding a good home for the toilet bowl planter. I'll bet somewhere, someone is tossing and turning that around in their dreams at this very moment.

Krupp's Home and Garden Décor crowds the corner of M21 and M13, aka 2011 Sheridan Avenue. It's open seven days a week; call (810) 621-3752 or (888) KRUPPS-1. You can order the $10,000 bronze fountain and other bits and pieces from www.krupps.com.

## WIMPS ONLY, PLEASE
### Lexington

The sign over the register reads, PRICES SUBJECT TO CHANGE ACCORDING TO CUSTOMER'S ATTITUDE. Wimpy's Place is all about attitude. The food almost seems secondary to the fun that exudes from the staff.

You may find the manager, Penny Nunn, and her crew harassing when they badger you to order more or call out to other diners that it's your fault orders are delayed because you're taking so long to make up your mind.

The menu is small, but then so is the interior, with room for only forty-nine customers, and that includes the dozen counter seats. Founded in 1987 by Jim and Cindy Gresock (just remember *greasy sock*), its mainstay is the burgers. The more you eat, the greater your chances of making it into the Belly Bomber Hall of Fame. All it takes is the consumption of twelve of Wimpy's burgers in an hour or less. Think it can't be done? Think again . . . at last count there were twenty-five members, with one good eater setting the record at eighteen.

Cases filled with Wimpy memorabilia line the walls. What doesn't fit in the case winds up in the Gresocks' basement. Word is that their home is crammed with every Wimpy product ever made, including a Popeye PacMan machine.

There's added incentive to chow down here—"a 25% Senior Citizen Discount . . .offered at 100 years of age, accompanied by both parents and must show photo ID."

Wimpy's Place opens every day for breakfast at 7:00 A.M.; closing time varies according to the season. It can be found at 7270 Huron Avenue in the heart of downtown Lexington. Call (810) 359–5450.

## *HERE COMES SANTA AND SANTA AND SANTA AND SANTA AND . . .*
### *Midland*

To be Santa is a privilege, not a job. That's the motto of the Charles W. Howard Santa School, the oldest Santa School in the world. It originated in 1937 in Albion, New York, but

*A school where there are absolutely no exceptions to the dress code*
*and clean-shaven faces are strictly forbidden.*

has been housed in Midland, Michigan, since 1987, when Tom
Valent became the school's third dean in history.

Valent says he "had a calling" to be Santa and wants to
share his enthusiasm for the jolly man in the red suit with the
rest of the world. He doesn't advertise and even shies away from
publicity for fear it may spoil some of the magic for children.

Yet each October, people from all over the world convene in
Midland's Santa House to hone their skills at playing St. Nick.
Besides Santa from Disney World and every mall imaginable,
there have been Santas from Sweden, Switzerland, Australia,
and England. The school has even done a tour of duty in

Greenland, being named the official host of the first World
Santa Claus Summit.

So what do people learn in Santa School? While the textbook
and basic principles remain the same as they were sixty-five
years ago, there has been updating. In addition to the heart
and spirit of Santa, students today learn how to sing, use sign
language, and give TV and radio interviews.

And cosmetics is another issue . . . the cost of playing Santa
isn't cheap. Equipment can run up to $4,000 with custom-made
hair and beard.

Tom's wife, Holly, has made sure that classes are all now
politically correct, with about 25 percent female attendees
learning how to portray Mrs. Santa Claus.

Santa School operates as a nonprofit organization. The cost
is $260 for three days . . . a real bargain for the opportunity to
bring a lifetime of happiness to children.

Classes are held in the Santa House, which is open to the
public free of charge from December 1 to December 28. The personification of Christmas, it's a veritable delight for the senses
and offers the opportunity to see the collection of 6-foot-tall
nutcrackers and other magnificent woodwork that Valent has
masterfully handcrafted.

The Valents are one amazing couple, who live and breathe
Christmas 365 days a year. With five children of their own,
they've added two reindeer to their household, Comet and
Cupid, both females. In fact, I'll share a secret. All of Santa's
reindeer are female because the males lose their antlers before
winter. And what would the sleigh look like without antlers on
the reindeer? It's true, Rudolph is really a girl.

The Santa House is located in downtown Midland on the
corner of Main and M20 (Isabella Road). For more information,
call (989) 631–0587 or log onto www.santaclausschool.com.

# CEILING TO FLOOR . . .
# CONFECTIONS AND MORE

**R**ight next door to Wimpy's (at 7272 Huron Avenue in Lexington) is the 117-year-old Lexington General Store, where I picked up my new favorite wall hanging reminding me, GOOD FRIENDS ARE LIKE FAT THIGHS, THEY ALWAYS KEEP IN TOUCH.

Your search for all those impossible-to-find candies of yesteryear will end right here. Baskets are on overload with Sen-Sen and bags of old-fashioned hard candy including horehound and sassafras, while your sweet tooth's memory will be tempted by oodles of penny candy, now inflationarily priced at 2 cents.

A general store where candy counters outnumber all
other goods.

### S MILE, S AY P INCONNING
#### P inconning

*inconning* is an Indian word meaning "place of potatoes." Then why is it designated as "Michigan's cheese capital" when no place in town makes cheese? Now, *cheese potato capital* I could understand.

To set the record straight, in 1915 local boy Dan Horn was doing a little cross-breeding of cheese recipes when he fell upon a mix that won the taste buds of both young and old. Patent-protecting his golden wedges from imitators, he assigned them the name of their birthplace: Pinconning.

Nowadays the formula remains the same, a cross between Colby and Cheddar, but the last plant here closed in 1995 so all the cheese wizardry is performed at an undisclosed location in the UP then hauled back to Horn's hometown for distribution to wholesale and retail markets.

The oldest of the brood is Wilson's Cheese Shoppe, founded in 1939 by Horn's daughter, who let the patent expire. Each year 125 tons of the partially homespun product goes out its doors; the aging process still takes up space in local coolers. With cheese, the older it gets, the more people like it. Like a memorable kiss, the measurement of perfection comes if it "melts in your mouth and bites your tongue at the same time."

Thanks to Wilson's, the rest of the country knows what the word *Pinconning* really stands for. Located at 130 North M13, Wilson's Cheese Shoppe is open 364 days a year, Merry Christmas, from 8:00 A.M. to 8:00 P.M. and occasionally later. Call (989) 879–2002.

## BROTHER, CAN YOU SPARE A DIME?
### Port Huron

*C*alling all international travelers! Here's your opportunity to experience two countries at one time, no matter what your budget. Just hop on the Blue Water Trolley. For one full hour, you'll be given a first-class introduction to forty-four of the top attractions in Port Huron, including a panoramic view of the Blue Water Bridge that leads to Canada. You'll be up-close and personal with freighters from all over the world as they pass through the St. Clair River on their way to Lake Huron. Filling you in on historical details and anecdotal stories of the city is a real live tour guide . . . No prerecorded narratives here. The fare for the journey? Just one thin dime.

That's been the price since 1986 when the trolley was first acquired by the Blue Water Area Transit, and there are no plans to raise it. Between early June and mid-October, about 2,200 travelers take advantage of the best bargain in town, possibly the world. You can do the math. There's not a lot of revenue there. Consequently, you may have to look at a few ads from places like Port Huron Paint or Bowl-A-Drome/Zebra Bar. But no one seems to mind when you can save some hard-earned dollars. There are reasons the rich are getting richer. Even Texas billionaire Ross Perot jumped on for the 10-cent jaunt when he was in town.

The thirty-two-seat trolley is available for special occasions on its off time and has been known to shuttle bachelorette, birthday, and wedding parties to and from destinations all across Michigan. You'll have to part with quite a few dimes for those services: Private charters are $160 an hour.

The trolley's hours of operation are Monday through Saturday 11:00 A.M. to 4:00 P.M. The trolley does not operate on Sunday. For more information and possible schedule changes, contact Blue Water Area Transit at (810) 987–7373.

## THOMAS ALVA EDISON: AN EDUCATOR'S NIGHTMARE
### Port Huron

Thomas Edison is quite likely the only person on earth to have been rejected by a school district, and years later have that same system name a school for him.

In 1854 Edison's family moved to Port Huron, when Tom was just seven. A bout with scarlet fever left him with a serious, yet misunderstood, hearing loss, prompting his teachers to find him dull, officially labeling him "addled." Infuriated, his mother tried two other schools, with no success, and subsequently concluded that homeschooling would be the best answer.

*Thomas Edison got his big break at this train depot, now dwarfed by the massive Blue Water Bridge.*

On October 10, 1965, the Port Huron Schools apparently had a change of heart, dedicating their newest school Thomas A. Edison Elementary.

In the early 1860s, Edison sold newspapers and snacks on the Grand Trunk Railroad, escaping boredom by building a printing press and mobile chemistry lab, igniting a fire on board during one of his phosphorus experiments.

All has been forgiven and in 2001, the Thomas Edison Depot Museum opened, allowing visitors a hands-on opportunity to create the world's next technological novelty in the same spot where the lightbulb first went off inside young Tom's mind.

The Depot Museum sits dwarfed under the Blue Water Bridge, north of Thomas Edison Parkway. (Isn't it funny how many things here are now named for this classroom failure?) It's open Wednesday through Sunday 1:00 to 4:30 P.M. every day during summer. Admission is charged. Call (810) 982–0891 or visit www.phmuseum.org.

## *TEAHOUSE OF THE SAGINAW MOON*
### *Saginaw*

**E**nter quietly and at your own risk of embarrassment as you comply with the ban on shoes. If ever you needed an excuse for a pedicure or a good reason to darn that hole in your sock, this is it: the traditional tea ceremony at the Japanese teahouse in downtown Saginaw.

Bred from a partnership with Saginaw's sister city, Tokushima, Japan, the teahouse is as authentic as it gets here in the States, incorporating classic Japanese architecture in its tongue-and-groove construction, without the use of one solitary nail. Unique in their sisterhood, both cities shared in the 1986 building costs and hold joint ownership of the land.

In Japan devotees spend a lifetime studying Teaism. In Saginaw you can spend an hour in an escape halfway around the world through the ceremonial high tea (Chado).

Only the best—the professed-healthy green tea powder, not the Bigelow bags we think are so rare, along with some sort of sweet—is delivered via a kimono-clad server.

When you're finished, a stroll through the tree-filled gardens will walk off the eighty-two calories consumed.

Daily tours of the teahouse at 527 Ezra Rust Drive are open to walk-ins. The ceremonial tea, held the second Saturday of each month, requires a reservation. Call (989) 759–1618 for more information.

## YOU SAY TOMATO . . .

*If you live in Michigan, do you call yourself a Michiganian or a Michigander? Your final answer may depend on how long you've been a resident. Lifers are the ganders, settlers are ganians. At least that's one theory.*

*Abraham Lincoln is blamed for starting the controversy with a prepresidential visit here in 1848 when he sarcastically referred to a political rival as a "Michigander."*

*We're the only state that can't seem to make up its mind. Lawmakers have tried forever to reach a compromise on our true identity, but so far, thanks to their indecision, we shall officially remain nameless.*

*Even the state's two largest newspapers can't agree . . .*

*The* Detroit News *takes the position we're Michiganians . . .*

*The* Detroit Free Press *calls us all Michiganders.*

*If that's the case, maybe women should be called Michigeese.*

## THE HEART OF THE PALM

# THE HEART OF THE PALM

**T**his is the pulse point of Michigan, where the main arteries filter through the diverse landscape, extending a rhythmic lifeline to the more than 9 million people in its grasp.

Lansing, the state's capital, was situated as close to a geographic center as possible at the time of its appointment, when arguments arose that it was not close enough to the Great Lakes. Perhaps no one realized then that no matter where you stand in Michigan, you're never more than 85 miles away from one of those five major bodies of water. Nowadays it's a toss-up whether we're better represented by Lansing's lugnut-topped chimney or the nineteen Tiffany of New York–designed chandeliers in the Capitol Building. (I vote for the chimney; it's easier to clean.)

A town originally named Milton witnessed a skirmish between a surveyor and a band of Potawatomis by the side of a rather obscure river. The surveyor must have been victorious since he changed the name of both the river and the town to Battle Creek, where you can have a grrrreat day chasing Tony the Tiger around at the world's longest breakfast table.

Either magic wands or pitchforks will get you in this neck of the woods. The town of Colon pulls in thousands for the country's largest magic convention even though there's not a single hotel room within miles of the city limits. And if that doesn't satisfy you, well, then you can go to Hell and back for a devil of a good time. It's just about an hour away.

And I'd be remiss in not mentioning the "heart" is the home of Michigan State University with its terra-cotta statue of Sparty (recently undergoing a bronze transformation possibly to deter the blue spray paint he's subjected to during the annual MSU–U of M football game) and prizewinning chocolate cheese, which honestly tastes much better than it sounds.

The curious heart of Michigan, housing Houdini, hairballs, and the Republican Party.

## A CITY FULL OF FLAKES
### Battle Creek

An accident in the spa's kitchen in 1894 is responsible for the industry that gives us our morning dose of snap, crackle, and pop. The Kellogg brothers were fast at work cooking wheat for their internationally famous Seventh Day Adventist health facility when they were called out unexpectedly. Their return to the kitchen found a batch of dried, stale grains, almost too flaky to do anything with. The brothers decided to bake the flaky grains and, to their amazement, the taste improved. Twelve months later the brothers had given away 4 million free samples of toasted cornflakes.

Today the Kellogg brand is the cornerstone for Cereal City, an interactive infotainment facility designed to replace tours of the seventy-four-year-old plant, which rising insurance premiums called to a halt in 1986. A simulated production line fills in with whiffs of cornflakes baking. "The Best to You" revue makes you feel like you're one of the children in *Honey, I Shrunk the Kids* with an ant's-eye view of the kitchen.

Although there are tons of other things to do, including snacking on a Froot Loops sundae, my personal favorite was the once-in-a-lifetime chance to be a "famous flake" (as they call it) with your photo on the front of a package of cornflakes. Not cheap at $20 per two-pack, it's still a novel souvenir, unless someone eats all the cereal inside and forgets to save the box.

Kellogg's celebrated its fiftieth anniversary in 1956 with the world's longest breakfast table, a continuing tradition the second Saturday every June. Filling up five city blocks in downtown Battle Creek, the festival feeds 65,000 people cereal, Pop-Tarts, doughnut holes, milk, bananas, and Tang from 8:00 A.M. to noon. Can you imagine what it would be like if they served fried eggs and bacon? For more information, contact the

*Flakes stand tall and never fall from this "rise 'n shine" tower,*
*evidence of a food source that is "perfectly balanced."*

Greater Battle Creek/Calhoun County Visitor and Convention
Bureau at (800) 397-2240.

Tony the Tiger prances around Cereal City Monday through
Friday 9:30 A.M. to 5:00 P.M., Saturday 9:30 A.M. to 6:00 P.M.,
and Sunday 11:00 A.M. to 5:00 P.M. Admission is charged. For
more information, call (269) 962–6230.

## WHEAT AND CORN REBORN

*B*y 1912 there were nearly a hundred companies in Battle Creek involved in manufacturing cereal. Of those Kellogg's, Ralston, and Post, a division of Kraft, still operate in the Cereal Capital of the World.

C. W. Post, once a patient at Kellogg's sanatorium, created his own product line featuring "Elijah's Manna." The name didn't click with the customers, so he changed it in 1904 to something more audibly pleasing . . . Post Toasties.

### LEAN ON ME
#### Chelsea

**S**eitz's Tavern is home to Michigan's longest-standing stand-up bar. Sound like double talk? Not at all. Oh sure, at 23 feet it's long, but it's unmatched anywhere because it never had and never will have any seats. At least not as long as it stays in the Seitz family, where it's been since 1916.

A jovial fellow with a welcoming smile, third-generation owner Randy Seitz is determined to maintain the tradition of resting only your feet and not your bottom. Besides being more conducive to conversation, the decision makes good business sense. Instead of accommodating only a dozen or so stools, throngs can get up-close and personal at the counter.

Any Saturday in June, entire wedding parties can be spotted making their descent for the $3.75 beef plate: three pieces of bread, beef, onions, and all the merriment a newlywed cocktail hour can provide.

Rubbing elbows with the unexpected is part of the charm—whether it's one of the regulars or a real live party animal, like the horse that stopped in for some waterin' down during the Centennial Celebration. Over the years hunters have been known to drop in with their conquests, some leaving long-lasting impressions such as the fella who burst in hurling his trophy bag of bull . . . frogs, leaving them to croak about, literally, for days.

Situated in the shadows of the silos of the Jiffy Food Mixes—you know, those popular cake mixes that have become staples in American households—third-generation customers now bring in their own children of all ages to experience this old-time legacy.

You'll find Seitz's Tavern at 110 West Middle Street in downtown Chelsea. Call (734) 475-7475. The hours are Monday through Saturday 7:00 A.M. until 1:00 or 2:00 A.M. Grandma Seitz's rule prevails today: closed on Sunday, allowing her to go to church and Grandpa to go fishin'.

## *MOREL MAJORITY EQUALS A MILLION PLUS*
### *Chelsea*

**M**ention fleshy fungi to Larry Lonik, his eyes light up bigger 'an saucers and, as befits his law school training, he's ready to hop up on a soapbox as a staunch advocate for the morel majority. To put it in simple terms, Larry looooves mushrooms and has likely handpicked more than anyone else in the world. With each ten-pound bag containing approximately 500

*At $110 per pound (dried), these truffles justify Larry Lonik's*
*wealth as the million-dollar mushroom man.*

to 600 morels, he figures he's harvested more than a million, a
backbreaking experience for the 6-foot, 7-inch Mr. Mushroom.

Growing up in Grand Rapids, Larry got caught by the
thrill of the hunt at an early age—six to be exact—when he discovered it was easier to scoop up morels in spring than it was
to find Easter eggs. That was nearly fifty years ago, and he
hasn't missed a picking season since.

He's traveled the globe in search of 'shrooms, and surprisingly the Arctic Circle ranks up at the top. Compare his worst
day there, rallying 150 pounds, to his best 80-pound day in
Michigan.

Although, according to Larry, a preponderance of spores
can be found sprouting over a 60-mile radius around Gaylord,

Michigan, he credits his kids with pinpointing the most humongous fungus from an unlikely location alongside the railroad tracks in Royal Oak: a 14-inch blond morel weighing one and a half pounds. That beauty and a pound of butter and you could have the whole neighborhood in morel heaven.

Larry's home base is Chelsea, but often shows up on Saturdays at the Royal Oak Farmer's Market on 11 Mile Road to sell any of his twenty different varieties of wild mushrooms. At $110, a one-pound bag of dehydrated morels translates to ten pounds of fresh. He's always ready to talk fungi: Call him at (877) 667–3518, or test the bacon-mushroom recipe from his Web site, www.morelheaven.com.

## *ALL HORSEPOWER CURBED HERE*

*Y*ou *can do almost everything in Coldwater without leaving the comfort of your car. With a flick of your turn signal, someone will hop to your service at Allen's Root Beer Drive-In. The menu is mostly reflective of its 1950 beginnings, though some updating has occurred—bubble gum and margarita are now among the eighteen varieties of slushes.*

*Kids are especially fond of the ice cream cones capped with a sugar-coated eyeball. If your pooch is spotted through the window, he'll be treated to a free doggy sundae complete with chewy bone topping.*

*Allen's Root Beer Drive-In dishes up delights at 378 West Chicago. Hours vary with the season. Call (517) 279–9048.*

### REEL-TIME RETRO
#### Coldwater

While many people think of the drive-in movie as a mecca for making out, my mother insisted she went there with someone she really didn't like, so no one else would see her with an embarrassing date. Whatever the reason, for nearly forty years people have continued to flock to the Capri Drive-in in Coldwater.

Founded in 1964 by John and Mary Magocs, today it remains somewhat of a big-screen version of *All in the Family.* On any given night you'll see current owners Tom and Sue Magocs and their three children among the crew bagging popcorn or cleaning the rest rooms. Their brood's total dedication to the movie biz is the reason they believe they're one of only eight drive-ins still in operation in Michigan.

It's always family-focused at the Capri, with close to 1,000 cars and trucks (the tallest to the back, please), packed with parents, kids, and pets. Before showtime Frisbees are flying through the air and out come the lawn chairs for a best-seat-in-the-house view of the star-filled sky. When the sun goes down, the "reel" magic begins, transforming acres of dirt into a Hollywood happening.

Named one of America's top 10 drive-in theaters in both the *New York Times* and *USA Today,* an evening here is a blast from the past, with two first-run double features projected on futuristic-sized 115-by-75 foot screens. Even Imax screens can't claim measurements of those proportions. What's really nifty about the whole setup is that everyone in your party doesn't have to watch the same movie. With the proper positioning you can enjoy the sight and state-of-the art stereo sound of one movie transmitted through your vehicle's radio, while someone else faces the opposite direction and receives the soundtrack of the alternative feature via portable radio. Talk about going to extremes to keep peace in the family.

The season begins weekends only in March, and has been known to get a snowy kickoff with windshield wipers going into overtime, and commences into full swing, seven days a week, May through October. Curtain time is at dusk, usually fifteen to twenty minutes after sunset, with the box office opening two hours prior—7:00 P.M. in spring, 8:00 P.M. in summer. A cafeteria-style snack bar stands ready to fill the needs of the fans with hot dogs, hamburgers, and cans of bug spray. Which reminds me . . . maybe they should start selling Windex since the night I viewed *Spiderman* he appeared to be splattered with a few too many lifelike creatures.

The Capri Drive-in Theater sits at 119 West Chicago Road. Call (517) 278–5628 or visit their Web site at www.capridrive-in.com. Admission charge.

## IF THE HEADSTONE IS WHITESTONE, IT'S BLACKSTONE
### Colon

Hollywood doesn't stand alone in issuing maps for celebrity grave sightings. The Colon Community Historical Society has put out a detailed schematic of nineteen of some of the world's finest magicians who have chosen to have Lakeside Cemetery as the scene of their "final act."

Viewings can take place without ever leaving the comfort of your car. Most markers are tall enough to spot while taking a leisurely drive through the seven straight-and-narrow pathways that will take you alongside such conjurors as Donald (Monk) Watson, who in vaudeville was teamed with Benjamin Kubelsky, later known as Jack Benny.

*Unexplainable images, invisible to the naked eye, have shown up on photos of this
"spirit-filled" tombstone, marking the graves of three Harry Blackstones.*

Fans of the 1950s show *Milky the Clown* will recognize the name Karrell Fox, whose epitaph fittingly reads IT WAS FUN.

Of course the most frequently visited grave site is that of Harry Blackstone, marked with a contemporary carved white stone. Three generations are buried here: Harry Sr., the first "Blackstone the Great"; Harry Jr., who became a magician only after producing Broadway's *Hair* and TV's *The Smothers Brothers Comedy Hour;* and Harry III, crushed by a broken car hoist while changing oil following his recent return home from the U.S. Marines.

Some of Blackstone's admirers are moved to tears, while others are moved to their wallets for coins, which are often seen lying at the base of the monument.

The last curtain call goes to "Little Johnny Jones," who left these words immortalized on his tombstone . . . NOW I HAVE TO GO AND FOOL ST. PETER.

Colon Lakeside Cemetery is located 1 mile west of the blinking light while you're looking east toward the village of Colon. You can pick up one of the maps at Abbott's Magic Company, 124 St. Joseph Street; (616) 432–3235.

## HOME OF HAIRBALLS AND THE TWO-HEADED CALF
### East Lansing

**M**ichigan State University originally started out as Michigan Agricultural College, and even today is referred to by some as MOO U. (I can say that since I'm an alumnus.). While the university is the largest in the state with more than 44,000 students, the agricultural school continues in full force with 171 head of cattle.

Obviously cows are a big part of the history of campus, and you'll find some engrossing forms of them at the MSU Museum. Founded in 1857, it's one of the oldest museums in the Midwest. Located right on campus, next to Beaumont Tower, it serves as a showcase for 2.5 million objects from all over the world. Yet it's never forgotten its farming roots, and currently boasts one of the largest collections of hairballs recovered from the stomachs of cows. The present assortment ranges from one the size of a plum to a whopper—dubbed the world's largest hairball—weighing in at four pounds, twelve ounces, measuring 9 inches across at its widest point, the size of a basketball. Val Berryman, the museum's curator of history, says hairballs form when there's a nutritional deficiency causing the cow to lose its appetite for normal food. So the animal licks itself, and the multicolored hairball is born.

Speaking of births, not all livestock are created equal. Sometimes two heads can be better than one, and the museum has a perfect example—a two-headed calf. Then there's the dwarf calf, donated to the museum in the early 1900s. The diminutive bovine stands a mere 1 foot tall, with legs of just a few inches and a body that extends only 2 feet in length. While no longer on permanent display, it makes "short" appearances at state fairs and other local venues.

The MSU Museum is next to the library on the campus of Michigan State. It's open Monday through Friday 9:00 A.M. to 5:00 P.M., Saturday 10:00 A.M. to 5:00 P.M., and Sunday 1:00 to 5:00 P.M. Admission is free. Call (517) 432–1472.

## A HEART-WORMING CLIFFHANGER
### Grand Ledge

Three hundred million years ago, Grand Ledge was a sea of salt water. Today what's left are layers of sandstone (the grand ledges) lining the banks of the Grand River, forming the biggest and best (and only) public rock climbing venue in the state.

History surrounds the site, although some of it is only accessible by ascending the 40-foot cliffs. (City officials say they're 60 feet; climbers tell a different story.) Some 12,000 people each year don their sporting gear and make the ascent in search of carvings, murals, and the rare flowering harebell plant, found only on bluffs and dunes.

An equally hearty number choose to keep their feet on the ground as spectators, either following the wooden-staired path or looking down on the action, watching as quietly as in a fishing tournament to see what's hooked at the end of the rope.

There's no question, cliffhangers are a rare breed with a softer side than their daredevil actions may lead you to believe. Take the group of climbers who one day, in a nesting area for cliff swallows, found a family of starving, motherless babies. Immediately they ceased their climb, digging up worms to hand-feed the little ones, repeating their nurturing routine each day for weeks until they were able to watch their "adoptees" fly away on their own to live happily ever after.

For the safest way to protect both yourself and the environment, it's best to get formal instruction. Vertical Ventures has been educating climbers in Grand Ledge's Oak Park for twenty years. Call them at (517) 336–0520 or click on their Web site: www.vertical-ventures.net. Oak Park with its sandstone cliffs can be reached off Front Street downtown. For more information, call the Grand Ledge Chamber of Commerce at (517) 627–2383 or visit www.grandledgemi.com.

## *THE ROAD TO HELL IS PAVED WITH . . .*
### *Hell*

"**E**xcuse me, could you please tell me how I go to Hell?" The clerk manages a chuckle. He hears it all the time. Fifteen minutes later I've arrived . . . in Hell, a three-store, 166-person town.

The only "Hell" anywhere on earth, its christening is credited to George Reeves, who in 1841 when asked for his opinion of the no-name enclave, brusquely replied, "You can name it Hell for all I care."

Today's demonic mastermind is John Colone, who gave up his day job as owner of a Chrysler dealership to become Odem Plenty, mayor of Hell and deed holder of Screams Ice Cream and Hell Country Store and Spirits and its official U.S. postal outlet. Every day anywhere from two to a hundred pieces of mail (many alimony checks) receive the official I'VE BEEN TO HELL postmark and a torching (a slight corner singeing) by the fires of Hell. On April 15 those numbers escalate substantially.

Enter the world of Screams Ice Cream through the 37-inch li'l devil door without bending over and a free cone is yours. However you do manage to get inside, though, your eyes will be immediately drawn to the genuine Transylvanian wooden coffin, where all the spooky sundae toppings sit, like bat droppings (chocolate chips), ghost poop (mini marshmallows), and buttersnot (butterscotch). Somebody must have had a fiendish frenzy labeling all those.

A Halloween gift shop adjoins so you don't have to go home without your favorite HELLUVA GOOD TIME T-shirt. Or a degree from Dam U. That's right, you, too, can become an on-the-spot graduate with a major in analology—awarded to those with great hindsight. The degree choices are limited only by your imagination, so be careful what you wish for.

*A year-round living Hell surrounds a Transylvanian coffin sundae bar at Screams Ice Cream and Gift Shop.*

Only in Michigan do you have the choice between Hell or Paradise; thanks to a local Boy Scout troop, the round-trip mileage between the two was unmasked at exactly 666 miles. Now that's a diabolically unnerving statistic. Those Boy Scouts obviously have way too much time on their hands.

A novel destination spot, especially in winter when you can use your Hell-freezes-over jokes. It's not the easiest to find, though all roads from Pinckney somehow lead you here. For more info, contact the Hell Chamber of Commerce at 4045 Patterson Lake Road, Hell, Michigan 48169, or (734) 878–0185. The Web site is as cunning as the town . . . www.hell2u.com or www.damu.com.

## BOY GOVERNOR

*Long before Boy George, Michigan was home of the "Boy Governor." In 1831 the governorship of the Michigan Territory was taken over by Stevens T. Mason when he was only nineteen years old!*

### PARTY WITH STANDING ROOM ONLY
#### Jackson

Jackson is probably not high on Al Gore's list of favorite places. For it was here, under a grove of shady oaks, that the Republican Party took its first steps.

A heated July 6, 1854, saw crowds of abolitionists overflowing from a convention hall, searching for a location large enough for to accommodate all the bodies, not to mention the egos. They found it in an area known as "Morgan's Forty," and began bustling under the trees for the purpose of establishing a third political party. With strong ties to the Underground Railroad, Jackson was an ideal site for the group of men to pass their first resolution declaring themselves "Republicans," professing to be descendants of Thomas Jefferson's Democratic-Republican Party, an oxymoron by today's standards.

Signs designate Jackson as the birthplace of the Republican Party, but city documents are a bit more vague, recognizing it only as the site of the first Republican convention.

In 1910 President Taft dedicated a boulder on the tiny corner lot now officially known as "Under the Oaks" with a handful of tall trees and a lonely park bench.

Once considered the outskirts, today it's in the heart of a quiet neighborhood. History buffs will love it, although there's not room to do much of anything. The park is open 7:00 A.M. to 10:00 P.M.; a sign says NO ALCOHOL. I guess politics in the Grand Old Party have changed.

## *HOT DOGS! POPCORN! LUGNUTS!*
### *Lansing*

**T**he road to the acquisition of a minor-league baseball franchise in Lansing was covered with more than just a few nuts and bolts. It was a journey with lots of bumps for team owner Tom Dickson, who'd nurtured a passion for the sport for years. His wife, Sherry Meyers, hoping to squelch his burning desire to own a team, wondered, "Why can't you just take piano lessons?" But together the former advertising execs succeeded in acquiring a franchise with a soon-to-be condemned stadium in Waterloo, Iowa. An attempt to move their new property to Springfield, Illinois, also failed. The third try, however, was the charm when in 1995 the city of Lansing was looking for an anchor for its new downtown facility.

A name-the-team contest quickly produced more than 2,000 entries, and on May 25, 1995, thanks to Lansing resident Jackie Borzich, the Lansing Lugnuts were christened. The town was outraged, placing over 145 opposing phone calls to the mayor's office while another 300 protests were logged at the stadium. It became a media frenzy, with David Letterman nationally ridiculing the team.

But by the time the first pitch was thrown out at Oldsmobile Park in April 1996, the public had had a change of heart and was ready to embrace its Lugnuts. Fans were filling the

11,714 seats, which included the general-admission "lawn" tickets where they could bring their own picnic basket and play Frisbee on the grass. They made their team No. 1 in merchandise sales among all minor-league baseball that year.

Watching a Lugnut game is unlike any other sporting event you've ever seen. It's nonstop entertainment with special attractions every half inning. You might be one of the lucky ones to be called on to do the chicken dance, or don a sumo wrestler's suit, or participate in the bungee run race with the Big Lug. And heads up . . . you never know when the hot dog cannon may be pointed in your direction.

Now an affiliate of the Chicago Cubs, the Lugnuts pull in more than 400,000 attendees a season and have already celebrated their 3 millionth fan. Tickets are available on-line at www.lansinglugnuts.com or by calling (517) 485–4500. The seventy-game season runs from April to September. Oldsmobile Park is located at 505 East Michigan Avenue in Lansing.

## *ABRACADABRA*

*T*he Marshall Library had been up for sale for more than two years when Elaine Lund realized she was outgrowing her magic museum. Fearful that the historical library might become a cluster of condos, in 2000 she bought it and converted it to the Lund Memorial Library. Today it houses the more than 15,000 books devoted to magic, and she's busy working on plans to host magicians' conventions there.

What may be even more amazing is how those 15,000 books traveled from the museum to the library, a distance of an eighth of a mile. In her midseventies Mrs. Lund carried every single one of them herself ("a few at a time") and lovingly placed them on the shelves.

## OPEN THE DOORS . . . POOF!
## MAGIC IN THE AIR
### Marshall

Imagine more than 15,000 books, 24,000 magazines, 600 show bills, 2,000 handbills, heralds, and window cards, 5,000 programs, 46,000 photos, hundreds of thousands of letters of correspondence and entertainers' scrapbooks . . . all on the subject of magic. They belong to one woman, Elaine Lund, who says, "I never dreamed I'd be in charge of all that paper."

But it's far more than paper. It's a private collection of everything magical, from the apparatus of legendary magicians to show announcements beckoning you to watch the "transformation of an orange to a lady." Originally started by Lund's late husband, Robert, the oldest item, a letter defining the occult, dates back to 1584.

With nearly a million pieces in total, the Lunds decided to share their "main attractions" with the rest of the world and began looking for a home for their "American Museum of Magic." They found it in Marshall in a bakery built in 1868. Purchasing the structure, they performed their own form of renovation magic and opened their doors to the public on April Fool's Day, 1978.

Taking center stage is their tribute to Harry Houdini with a platform filled with gadgets once used by the famous showman. You'll be able to touch and feel the renowned milk can from which he never failed to escape, including the mastodon eight lever locks used to fasten him inside. With a little prodding, you just might be able to get Mrs. Lund to let you in on the secret of how it all works.

Harry Blackstone was a friend of Bob Lund's, and the museum certainly has evidence of that. His complete set of traveling cases with his orange identification markings are stored in the basement. Blackstone, whose real name was Boughton, shortened to Bouton, had a place on a lake in Colon, Michigan, referred to as Magic Capital of the World.

All in all it's a magical experience with more than a few eerie coincidences. Elaine Lund says she got into the magic scene because she "married the wrong man." However, don't rule out influence from another source. You see, she was born in Grace Hospital in Detroit on October 25, 1926. Houdini died in that very hospital on October 31, 1926. As Lund herself states, "My mother, Harry, and I were all there at the same time."

The American Magic Museum is free and is open by appointment only, but Mrs. Lund says she's given tours from 5:00 A.M. to midnight. So it's okay to call anytime. The phone number at the museum is (269) 781–7666. Some say "666" is the sign of the devil. Mrs. Lund says they did not order that number—"it just happened."

## CAPITAL LOSS CARRIES OVER

*With the length of time it takes for politicians to come to agreement, it's a wonder Michigan has a capital city even today. Detroit served temporarily in that capacity, with just about every city in contention when the final vote came up in 1847.*

*Lobbying was fierce and confidence was high, at least in Marshall, Michigan. The town believed so strongly it'd be the permanent choice that it erected a governor's mansion, which still stands without ever having a governor in residence.*

*The State House had thirteen site selections before agreeing on Lansing Township, but the Senate voted fifty-one times before final confirmation. According to one account, when the last tally was taken, Marshall lost its bid by just one vote.*

## STAMP HIM PRINCE OF 49068
### Marshall

**M**ike Schragg is not a salesman by profession, yet his constant level of enthusiasm could make anyone find exhilaration in something as mundane as a postage stamp. Which is exactly what he does, often seven days a week, as postmaster of Marshall and founder and curator of the Postal Museum. Anything, and I do mean anything, having to do with getting the mail through is either wedged solidly into his memory bank—you can't send a human being, even if he's under the seventy-pound weight restriction; chickens are okay if they can go two days without water—or on display in the basement of the architecturally inspiring Greek Revival post office.

A lifetime fascination with postal peculiarities came to fruition in 1987 when the museum opened its doors stocked with Mike's personal collection, along with donated artifacts from fellow hobbyists. Leather postcards, stagecoach mail pouches, old-fashioned postmarking tools (which when demonstrated will awaken even the most lethargic listener), and some great trivia tales are all part of the tour.

I never realized, but I'm glad I know now, that women were responsible for the invention of home delivery. During the Civil War they'd bombard the post office in search of letters from their loved ones, often begging so much that the postmaster told them to leave; as consolation he told them that if a letter appeared, he'd send someone out to personally deliver it.

Mike's crowning glory is a 1931 Model A Ford mail truck in mint condition, which he gratifyingly chauffeurs in parades and special events, like the January 2001 inauguration of President Bush. After a 5:00 A.M. stage call, he finally rolled by the prez sometime around 4:00 in the afternoon. Patience, it's just one of his saintly qualities.

*Mike Schragg behind the wheel of his dream come true: a 1931 Model "A" Ford mail truck, now housed in its own custom-designed garage.*

A long list of stellar individuals preceded him in his current position, including a banker, a doctor, a newspaper publisher, and a stagecoach operator. You see, postmaster of Marshall is Mike Schragg's day job. At night you can find him downtown managing Win Schuler's restaurant with the same zip that's become his personal code of conduct.

The Postal Museum is located at 202 East Michigan Avenue. If you'd like to schedule a tour (by appointment only) or have an old set of stamps you'd like to drop off, call (269) 781–2859. Free admission.

# THE CHEESE GOD

**W**oody Dunham's license plate labels him the chezgod. His family-owned and -operated Caleb Dunham Cheese Co. offers a plant tour in which you can watch 140 quarts of cheese spread roll off the conveyor belt at one time with the grace of a Lucy and Ethel routine. The plant operates only three days a week, turning out nine different varieties, like "lumpy chunky Cheddar cheese with chives," so it's best to call ahead— (269) 789–0840. It's found at 1616 Pratt Road, about a mile from downtown Marshall.

## "TUBA, OR NOT TUBA"
### Okemos

**W**illiam White has treasured the tuba since he first started playing one when he was nine years old. Actually he began his musical career on a sousaphone, a circular tuba shaped so that one can carry it while marching. Today he's the proprietor of the Travelers Club International Restaurant and Tuba Museum. That's quite a mouthful, but then tuba players are probably used to that.

*Ever wonder what a squished tuba looks like? A steamroller did the job on this one, now cemented alongside the entrance to the tuba museum.*

Situated in a former hardware store built in 1950, the museum-restaurant is home to more than sixty tubas, the oldest dating back to 1870. It's a horn blower's heaven with all the large bass instruments, most in playing condition, and vintage tuba photos filling the walls. Here you'll see the world's only remaining "Majestic Monster," a double E flat Helicon tuba. Even though it was built in Austria circa 1915, it's a true Michiganian, having been a fixture of the UP's Iron Mountain Community Band.

While the musical aspect will get you inside, it's the food that will keep you here even longer. For more than twenty years, White and his partner, Jennifer Brooke, have been offering guests a traveling menu. Both say they love to cook feasts of ethnic food but don't like to cook the same thing too often. Hence the menu changes monthly, focusing on different regions of the world. One month you could be savoring the tastes of India with delicacies like lime potatoes. The next month your choice would be something with a Mexican flair.

*Totally eclectic* is a fitting description for the food and folly here. Don't be surprised if you see and hear members of the Michigan State University marching band come parading through at any time. It's all part of one man's devotion to the tuba. Just outside the building is White's Tribute to Tubas, an original artistic creation that honors all the "tubes" that have met their untimely demise after being run over on the field by football players. As an everlasting tribute, White took an old tuba, had a steamroller go over it several times, and then enshrined it in cement.

Traveler's Club International Restaurant and Tuba Museum is located at 2138 Hamilton Road, Okemos. It's open seven days a week at 8:00 A.M. For more information, call (517) 349–1701.

## NEXT STAGECOACH STOPS HERE
### Onsted

In 1965 Fred Bahlau was looking for a place to display his wife's lifelong hobby, which then added up to 10,000 antiques. Hoping the public would appreciate them as much as she did, he opened up Stagecoach Stop USA, not unlike a stationary antiques road show before its time. With a 50-cent admission charge, there were few takers: Fred admits, "We lost our fannies."

In search of the return of their hind sides, Fred and Doris decided to go all-out, filling their seventy-five acres with a blacksmith shop, sawmill, sheriff's jail, and anything else that was reminiscent of the Old West. Sprinkle it all with working demonstrations and an occasional staged gunfight and they had a winner on their hands.

Then in 1975, Fred got a call from Ed Lowe, the creator of Kitty Litter, whose own plans for establishing a western town in nearby Jones had fallen through. He now was searching for a buyer for one of his prized possessions: President Eisenhower's railroad car, a pre-aeronautical version of *Air Force One*. Remembering fondly as a young serviceman the day in 1944 when Ike and Winston Churchill had walked right in front of him, Fred soon had cranes unloading the choo-choo at its current home, where it waits for visitors to walk through, right next to the fudge shop.

Antiques now number in the 60,000 range, matching the annual attendance figures, which separates this place from other fantasy attractions. With so many authenticities already on hand, nothing had to be manufactured in some design studio (excusing the giant Paul Bunyan).

And to accommodate the hungry overflow, Fred and Doris own the Golden Nugget right across the street. It's easy to spot the joint. Over the entry stands a 10-foot cow, sporting a derby on its head and a chunk of gold 'round its neck.

The season for Stagecoach Stop USA runs from Memorial Day through Labor Day. Open weekends September and October. Closed Monday. It opens at 10:30 A.M. and shuts down for the day somewhere between 5:00 and 6:30 P.M. Find it in the heart of the Irish Hills at 7203 U.S. Highway 12. Contact (517) 467–2300 or visit www.stagecoachstop.com. Admission charge for adults and children four years and older. Special group rates available.

## GIZZARD CITY, USA
### Potterville

"**A** face like a gizzard"—in Potterville that's a compliment. It all started when Potterville Days, a long-standing festival in this community of 2,100, wasn't bringing in the crowds like it used to. Recognizing the need for change, chairman Jo Lehman decided to capitalize on the No. 1 selling menu item since 1960 at Joe's Potterville Inn: chicken gizzards, pressure-cooked, deep-fried, and served with cocktail sauce.

Now each year on the third weekend in June, the Gizzard Festival has 16,000 waiting in front of seven vats of boiling oil for more than an hour to gobble up 2,000 pounds of digestive organs. Well, maybe not all 16,000 partake. You either love 'em or abhor 'em. It's only hearsay that they've got the same texture as a mushroom; my cholesterol can't cope with the fried part.

If you're one of those who can't get enough of the "delicacies," you're an ideal candidate for the gizzard-eating contest. Whoever can put away two pounds in the least amount of time becomes the champion gizzard guzzler (a surefire résumé booster). The time to beat is that of Brian Rock of Potterville, who in 2002 spent just four minutes and eleven seconds stom-aching stomach parts, while fifteen other contestants were passing bottles of Tums.

As the Gizzard Parade passes by, everyone smiles and waves at the Gizzard Princess—there really is such a person, but only in Potterville. You have to admit the whole idea can be either humorous or repulsive, depending on your level of taste. The less adventurous gastronomes are the ones sporting the T-shirts reading WE CHICKENED OUT.

For festival information, call Jo Lehman at (517) 645–2313. For gizzard tasting year-round, stop by Joe's Potterville Inn, 110 South Main Street; (517) 645–2120. Six days a week they open at 10:30 A.M., Sunday, it's noon. Closing time depends on the crowd.

## THE COVERED BRIDGE OF IONIA COUNTY
### *Smyrna*

**M**ichigan's oldest covered bridge sits proudly over the Flat River in Keene Township. Built in 1869, White's Bridge was named for a prominent pioneer family. Jared N. Breese and J. N. Walker took just eighty-four days to construct the 120-foot-long structure. But the building wasn't without contro-versy. First, the people of Smyrna were short on cash, so the contract called for deferred payments—$1,000 due in 1870, with another $700 paid the following year. However, there was unhappiness over some auger holes in the planks, so $25 was deducted from the bill.

Yet the bridge stands mighty today, with only some minor repairs to the siding and a new cedar shingle roof. Otherwise, it's been in continuous use by vehicle traffic for more than 130 years.

*"If the bridge is short, a kiss will do; if it's long there's time for a hug or two." Let your imagination fill in the affairs on this 120-foot bridge.*

Traditionally covered bridges were used for a variety of happenings outside of travel; including hosting concerts, church suppers, and even weddings. Yes, the romantic aura of the covered bridge lives on today. The rough timbers provided a perfect place to carve symbols of love for all eternity.

Of course there's the popular superstition associated with covered bridges . . .

Make a wish and hold your breath as you go through. Hold it all the way and your wish comes true.

At 120 feet long, a trip through White's Covered Bridge could just make all your dreams become reality.

White's Covered Bridge stands on Whites Bridge Road over the Flat River, south of 4 Mile Road in Keene Township.

NOT-SO-WILD WEST

# NOT-SO-WILD WEST

**C**hances are good you're from conservative west Michigan if you've ever worn wooden shoes while dancing in the street, or have gone to church twice on Sunday, or your first job was picking blueberries. This side of the state is true blue, with a crop that supplies 45 percent of all of blueberries consumed in America. In South Haven there's even a whole store devoted to the reported cancer-fighting brain booster. The Blueberry Store—with goodies like blueberry salsa, blueberry popcorn, and blueberry coffee—would keep a blueblood pacified for a lifetime.

The area has turned out its share of bluebloods, with President Gerald Ford claiming Grand Rapids as his hometown (he was two when he moved here). *X-Files* star Gillian Anderson graduated from high school in Grand Rapids, as did Jim Bakker of PTL Club fame . . . known for borrowing money. Perhaps *PTL* came from the words he heard even then from his teenage lenders—Pay the Loan.

Muhammad Ali has called Berrien Springs home since the mid-1970s, when he purchased an estate-sized farm along the St. Joseph River previously owned by one of Al Capone's cronies. On any given day the Great One could be next to you in line at the only McDonald's in town.

The picturesque sand dunes along Lake Michigan have caused a convergence of smartsy-artsy folks, so many that the Saugatuck/Douglas area has come to be known as the Art Coast with an endless stream of galleries. Where else would you find public rest rooms adorned with impressionist paintings?

A worldly sampling awaits with Singapore, a once booming lumber town now buried in the sand waiting for the wind to blow just right to unveil a glimpse of a wall of chimney left behind from the 1800s. And of course there's Holland, where they still wash down the streets with their dancing feet in wooden shoes.

Michigan's west: tamed, yet curiously unspoiled.

## TREE HOUSE STUMPS ALL
### Baldwin

William Overholzer, the personification of patience and perseverance, spent twenty-two years building his home and each of the 200 pieces of furniture in it, all out of wood. His admiration for the white virgin pine wouldn't allow him to cut any trees down, so he would row down the Pere Marquette River while his wife—his former third-grade teacher and twenty-four years his senior—looked for ideal stumps to carve.

What Overholzer did with their discoveries is almost beyond belief. A fallen tree would be painstakingly handcrafted (no power tools here) into a chair—a month's work apiece—a rifle stand, a poker table, or another utilitarian work of art. One lucky log became a rocking chair so perfectly balanced, it swings fifty-five times with only a single push. Sandpaper and glue were all homemade; instead of nails, wooden pegs became fasteners. From beginning to end, the entire process was all natural.

That carried through to the accessories as well. A turtle's shell became an ashtray. To differentiate checkers, one set was left plain, the other boiled in blackberry juice. Seventy tons of uncut stones from five Michigan counties stacked into a fireplace.

The focal point of this one-oversized-room house is a 700-pound stump. After four years of whittling away 300 of those pounds, the stump became an incredible dining table, with drawers perfectly hollowed out for silverware. Henry Ford heard about this massive marvel and in 1940 made an offer of $50,000, only to have it rejected.

No amount of money could make Overholzer, a hunting and fishing guide, part with his beloved pines. Today his home is referred to as "Shrine in the Pines." An only child (his father was eighty when he was born) with no heirs, when he died in 1952 at age sixty-two, he willed everything to Boysville in Clinton. With the assistance of the Society for the Preservation of Shrine of the Pines, the house with the world's largest collection of rustic pine furniture is now open for the public to enjoy, just the way the artist and his wife always wanted it to be.

Surrounded by pines, naturally, the cabin and gift shop are located on M37, 2 miles south of Baldwin. Tours are offered seven days a week, May 15 through October 15, Monday through Saturday 10:00 A.M. to 6:00 P.M., Sunday 1:30 to 6:00 P.M. There is an admission fee. Call (616) 745–7892.

Be sure to take a walk down to the river. The setting is equally as heavenly as the "shrine."

## THE OLD BALL GAME, NOW EVEN OLDER
### Benton Harbor

A 1,000-member religious commune, an amusement park, and a world-class baseball team: At one time those were defining attributes of the House of David. The membership today has dwindled to eight. The train rides are long gone. But the spirit of America's favorite pastime has been given new life.

A little history lesson to comprehend the magnitude of the team that once was. Dubbed by Satchel Paige "the Jesus Boys" for their long hair and beards, the House of David ball club went into the record books for signing Jackie Mitchell in 1933, the first female professional player, who came with the unprecedented distinction of being the only pitcher to strike out—in the same inning—both Lou Gehrig and Babe Ruth. On April 7, 1930, they initiated night baseball with a game in

*Constructed in 2000, the absence of modern conveniences makes this new baseball stadium a remarkable venue.*

Independence, Kansas. The guys minus the gal (she left after reportedly being asked to play an exhibition inning while riding a donkey) went on to decades of notoriety as successful athletes until the 1950s, when things started to decline and the team struck out permanently.

Baseball, though, is again on the upswing here, with the 2000 formation of a new team, the House of David Echoes, who play by pre–Civil War rules set in 1858. They use handmade, hand-sewn balls; there are no gloves, but also not as many "ouches" as you would think. If a ball is caught on the first bounce, it's an out.

Vintage baseball is catching on with a number of traveling teams on the scene throughout Michigan: the Rochester Hills Grangers, Midland Great River Hogs, and Berrien Springs Cranberry Boggers, to name a few.

Some things don't change. A new team needs a new stadium, and while it's not Comerica Park, the historically accurate Eastman Field accomplishes just what it set out to do . . . take fans back 150 years, with rustic log seating and very strict rules. Footwear at all times, no arguing, and no cursing. Which must please the umpires more than anyone.

The House of David has opened up its mega-acre historical facility at the corner of Britain and Eastman for public tours, June through September, Saturday and Sunday from 1:00 to 5:00 P.M. Admission charge. Allow about two hours. For more information on tours, vintage baseball, or their vegetarian banquets, call (269) 926–6695 or (269) 925–1601, or log onto www.maryscityofdavid.org.

### D O U B L E   D O S E   O F   P I C K L E M A N I A
### *B e r r i e n   S p r i n g s*

**I**f one pickle festival a year is a good thing, then two must be even better. Or at least this made sense to the organizers, who found out the hard way that some things get lost in the transition between seasons. Like those appealing chocolate-covered gherkin pickles served at the Christmas Pickle Fest. One crunchy bite in crispy December and your eyes will water for hours. In July, though, those babies are as messy as a newborn's diaper.

But why pay homage to pickles here at all, where there's not a single pickle plant in sight? The chairman of the Pickle Promotion Board Executive Committee, Chuck Voytovick, has a

*Cool as a cucumber. That's how this giant dill pickle
must feel during his transformation into
Saint Pickolos.*

logical explanation: "We wanted to have a festival and all the other fruits and vegetables in the area were already taken." Which left them, so to speak, in a pickle.

There is a hint of sane rationale. To Germans (and there are a few in the area), a pickle is a prized possession, with their Old World custom of hiding one each year in the Christmas tree, resulting in an extra present from Santa for the child who first spots it. That's why packs of pickle ornaments to perk up the tree can be procured from peddlers in pretty much every part of town.

Summertime provides the opportunity to partake in activities conducive to outdoor consumption, like the now famous pickle fling. On the sidelines are those who get a kick out of watching an official No. 2 sized pickle being flung down the street to land with a giant *splat*. The world record for pickle-flinging is believed to have been set right here in Berrien Springs, squishing in at 297 feet.

For a quarter you can be a player in the pickle smash: Pick up a mallet, and wham! Instant pickle juice. Someone thought it would be a good idea to turn this into a contest, but mashed pickles were found to be too hard to judge. There's the pickle toss, pickle Bozo Bucket game, pickle sack race . . . just about anything you would never want to do with a pickle can be done here.

Parades cap off each biannual celebration, with the hands-down favorite the last float of the year . . . a giant pickle dressed in a red velvet suit affectionately known to all as "Saint Pickolos."

The summer pickle festival happens the last Sunday in July; Christmas pickle fest is the first Sunday in December. For more information, call (269) 449–2910.

## GOURMET GATOR TO GO
### Berrien Springs

While most little boys had visions of growing up to become a fireman or a doctor or a rock star, Gary Zick, at the age of ten, stood up and told the world exactly what he was going to be: a sausage maker. Even in college, everyone knew him as the kid with the rows of ham and homemade sausage hanging like lanterns throughout his dorm room.

And today he's living out his dreams as owner of Zick's Specialty Meats and Sausages, utilizing the Old World techniques he learned as a kid in his dad's grocery store from German experts in the fine art of mincing meats. Desirous of a niche, he went wild—as in wild game and other exotic species—and now grinds 2,000 pounds a day into twenty-six different varieties of Buffalo Bob snacks. Except they're not all buffalo. Among the alien choices are venison, elk, ostrich, wild boar, duck, and pheasant.

More alligator goes out the door than anything else. There must be something in the taste of those scaly reptilian legs and tail that causes people's mouths to water so much they can't wait to sink their teeth into the meat and rip off a hunk.

Gary loves watching people's reactions when he offers his anonymous "try it, you'll like it" samples. When he gets the thumbs up, he owns up. You've been taken in by a bite of kangaroo.

Zick's Market is open Monday through Friday 9:00 A.M. to 5:00 P.M., Saturday until 1:00 P.M., except in summer when they close all weekend. You can view the mixers whipping up pemmican—a meat-and-dried-fruit medley second only to fruitcake—at 215 North Mechanic Street. Mail orders are available by calling (269) 471–7121 or through their Web site, www.buffalobobsnacks.com.

# CATS GIVE PAWS UP TO CLAY

*LOCAL GUY SET TO MAKE MILLIONS SELLING CRAPPY IDEA.* That could have been the foresighted headline of the Cassopolis newspaper back in 1947 when Ed Lowe fell upon a concept that was about to change the way American cats conduct their business.

As a salesman for industrial absorbents, Ed was one day approached by a woman upset over the messy ashes in her cat's box, which caused sooty paw prints to leave their mark everywhere. He casually suggested using clay, which had a more spongelike quality. Both she and the cat loved it, and there were high hopes that others would, too.

Filling ten paper bags with five pounds of clay pellets, Ed traipsed down to the pet store and tried to peddle them for 65 cents. The owner was doubtful anyone would pay that much, so entrepreneurial Ed told him to give away the product he had hastily labeled "Kitty Litter."

Ed Lowe Industries went on to become one of those overnight successes that took decades of hard work. Always on the prowl for ways to make his goods better, at one point he built his own "cat house," employing 120 felines who were called upon twenty-four hours a day by researchers assessing their every movement.

Ed passed away on October 4, 1995, but his wife remains actively involved overseeing their own 2,500-acre "city" replete with a church, farmhouse, and five train cars.

One more incidental . . . let's clarify those millions referred to earlier. In 1990, just before Ralston Purina purchased the company, sales of Kitty Litter were raking in more than $200 million a year. At least one tabby thinks that's not too shabby.

The Ed Lowe Foundation offers support services for budding entrepreneurs. To get all the scoop, call (800) 232-LOWE—that's (800) 232-5693. Address all inquiries to P.O. Box 8, Cassopolis, Michigan 49031-0008.

## THE GREAT CARUSO LIVES IN CHOCOLATE
### Dowagiac

**M**ost restaurateurs love to boast about their homemade soups, which have been simmering all day for maximum flavor. Caruso's, however, is brutally honest right on its menu—"Campbell's soup every day"—given credence by the towering stack of cans at the front door.

Whatever you think of this tell-it-like-it-is attitude, it's been a successful formula from the first day of business as Caruso's Candy Kitchen on September 22, 1922. The recipes, the Italian marble soda fountain, they've passed the test of time.

The anxious anticipation I had for a taste of the olive nut sandwich I'd heard about turned quickly to disappointment when I learned that it was temporarily "out of stock." Either there had just been a mad rush or no one had ordered one in so long they didn't bother inventorying it. In any case, I guess "olive" without it.

Life is short . . . eat dessert first—no problem. Zeroing in on one of the thirty-two specialty sundaes will be, though. How do I choose between a mucky-sounding green river syrup filling a dish with crushed cherries and vanilla ice cream to resemble the Italian flag, and something called a "sauerkraut sundae"?

Maybe it'll be easier to settle on a selection from the candy case. Everything in it is homemade: chocolate pizza, chocolate toolboxes, chocolate greeting cards, chocolate cows. That's it. I'll take a milk chocolate cow to fill my dairy needs for the day.

Caruso's, with no rest room even for patrons, is in the heart of downtown Dowagiac. The 1899 building is in the middle of the block at 130 South Front Street. For hours, call (269) 782–6001.

# READY . . . SET . . . P'TOOEY
## *Eau Claire*

**E**very Fourth of July, fans clamor for the best seat in the bleachers, slathering on the sunscreen and pulling out the binoculars in preparation to enjoy an afternoon of . . . watching people spit. A three-decade-old competition, viewed by some as the pits, others as "spitacular" . . . it's the International Cherry Pit Spit Contest. Try to say that ten times fast.

The sport grew somewhat by accident out of a seed in the mind of Herb Teichman, owner of the 160-acre Tree-Mendus Fruit Orchards, when he nonchalantly tossed a couple of cherries to some restless youngsters waiting for their parents, drew a line in the sand, and challenged them to cross over it with a hefty sputter. Give any kid a legitimate reason to spit and you've got a real winner on your hands.

So Herb installed a 100-by-20-foot blacktop court, set some rules—no foreign objects in the mouth, denture racks provided for those wishing to remove their teeth—and it wasn't long before Peter Pans from across the globe were entering the "spitting box" with all the pageantry of the World Wide Wrestling Federation. Now athletes known as Phantom of the Orchard and the Sultan of Spit sashay through the audience. But it's the opulent entrance of Rick "Pellet Gun" Krause high atop a purple Harley tossing out his autographed trading cards who really drives fans berserk. As the eleven-time winner of the world championship, an unparalleled record in the annals of international cherry pit competition, Krause has reason to be braggadocious.

There must be a gene that determines if you'll be a distance spitter. Like father, like son. It's Rick's son, Brian "Young Gun" Krause, who holds the official Guinness World Record of 72 feet, 11 inches, set in 1998.

Practice is encouraged here anytime, although the winds appear more favorable on the front qualifying court. For home use, there's the "Cherry Pitspitter Training Kit" complete with rule book, cherry pits, and an official measurement cord.

Giving pits the heave-ho isn't the only activity down on this farm. You can walk, rent a golf cart, or hop the "folkswagon" for a U-pick experience among the 10,000 trees. And don't worry about the pits. Herb has a one-ton-an-hour cherry pitter that'll do the tough stuff for you.

Time of year dictates the type of fruit. In addition to cherries, peaches, apricots, nectarines, plums, and more than 250 varieties of apples—including the one-of-a-kind apple grown in a sack—are also available. Tree-Mendus Fruit Orchards and Country Store is located on 9351 East Eureka Road. For information on tours, their rent-a-tree program, or the pit spitting contest, call (269) 782–7101 or visit www.treemendus-fruit. com.

A couple of last-minute pointers from the pros: Take a big deep breath and make sure your tongue is rolled up nice and tight around the pit for a hearty cannon effect.

## TOMBSTONE TERRITORY
### Eau Claire

"**B**ring back the good ol' days," exclaimed Elwell Hoyt in the late 1800s. Frustrated with all the newfangled, high-tech gadgets like electricity, the wealthy businessman decided to generate his own return to primeval times by building a log cabin devoid of any "modern" conveniences.

The 25-by-32-foot structure was built without nails, and had just one window for a peek of daylight. Furniture, all made out of coarse hickory, was kept to a bare minimum. The bed was

*The Hoyt family will always feel right at home in this
cemetery, alongside their monumental limestone cabin.*

three-cornered, brooms were made to order out of a solid stick
of hickory, and no matches ever touched a candle wick, prefer-
ring, instead, a stroke of flint.

Elwell couldn't bear the thought of parting with his home
here on earth, so before he departed for good, he commissioned
a log cabin tombstone to be hand-carved out of limestone and
ready when the call came. (If he'd had a cell phone, the call
might never have gotten through.) The monument was placed
on his grave in 1905 with two "log" headstones on either side,
one for him, the other for his wife, Hattie, who died in 1919.

Many a curious log cabin enthusiast has cast an eye on the Eau Claire Cemetery, which has become a regular stop on Log Cabin Day festivities.

The impact of Elwell's thinking proves that he really was never behind the times at all, realizing early the value that it took the rest of us almost a century to appreciate. I wonder if anyone a hundred years from now will speak kindly about programmable VCRs.

The cemetery is on M62, just east of the village of Eau Claire before the M140 intersection. Virginia Handy, cofounder of the Log Cabin Society of Michigan, can answer any questions. Contact her at (269) 925–3836 or www.qtm.net-logcabincrafts.

## *Did You Know?*

*M*ichigan is the only place in the world with an annual statewide Log Cabin festival. Under proclamation of Governor James Blanchard on June 15, 1989, "the last Sunday of June of each year shall be known as Log Cabin Day."

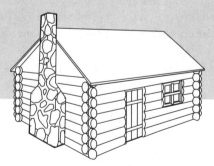

## Do Not Feed the Animals—They're Already Stuffed
### *Fennville*

HER NAME IS BETTY. 1930–1937. SHE LIVED IN CHICAGO. Those are the words on the sign hanging from the neck of the dog cradled in a sleigh just past the cash register at Crane's Pie Pantry Restaurant. Good thing she's near the exit door so she won't cause any folks to lose their appetite. That's because Betty is stuffed. Been stuffed for years, by the hands of a skilled taxidermist.

One of the eight full-time bakers on staff had an aunt who was awarded custody when Betty's owner died. Growing weary with the constant vacuuming she required, the aunt quickly found her mutt a new home as a curious attraction for patrons. Betty wasn't alone for long. Around the corner are a couple of Plymouth Rock chickens that apparently paid a visit to the same stuffer. If Roy Rogers could have Trigger packed for perpetuity, this doesn't seem all that unusual.

A sense of humor and an irresistible fervor for antiques have become trademarks for Bob and Lue Crane, owners of Crane's Pie Pantry. One Christmas, Lue had a tough time deciding what to buy for her husband, the man who had everything. So she decided to get him another woman and wrapped up an antique mannequin.

For years the couple had run their family's centennial fruit farm. When the restaurant opened in 1972, hours were spent perfecting Mom's pie recipe for larger quantities. Success didn't come easily, with the first batch "ending in the dumpster." But since then hundreds of pies-in-the-sky have been forklifted from the kitchen in the old hayloft down to the first-floor bakery case.

*She may look bright-eyed and bushy-tailed, but Betty's bark is gone forever.*

The Cranes have left no apple unturned with menu items of apple butter bread, apple butter ice cream, and apple-cidersicles. This is also the one place in the state, maybe in all of America, where you won't find any soda pop on the menu. The beverage of choice is apple cider, served chilled or hot, with free refills year-round.

The notice out back reminds us STRESSED IS DESSERTS SPELLED BACKWARDS. Stay calm, your sweet tooth won't be tempted here by any hint of "Apple Betty."

Crane's Pie Pantry Restaurant, Bakeries and Cider Mill are in the back of 6054 124th Avenue (M89), 2 miles west of town. Out front sit the packing house and freezers, so don't be discouraged if you pass by. Hours vary with the season. Call ahead at (269) 561–2297 or consult their Web site, www.cranes piepantry.com.

### THREE TUNES (OR MORE) IN A FOUNTAIN
#### Grand Haven

About an hour before dusk, crowds congregate in and around the Municipal Marina: locals sprawled on blankets, tourists ascending the waterfront grandstand, all anxiously awaiting the first sign of life from the Grand Haven Musical Fountain. Promptly at 10:00 P.M.—times vary according to the sunset—the throbbing percussion from *2001 Space Odyssey* vibrates through the air, followed by a booming baritone bellowing from the other side of the Grand River channel, "I am the voice of the musical fountain."

The moist mouthpiece continues, announcing the evening's playbill, *Let's Walk*. Okay, it may be hokey, but the audience loves it.

For the next twenty-five minutes, thousands of spectators feast on a free synchronized performance of light and sound with more than 40,000 gallons of water choreographed to twist, turn, and kick 100 feet skyward with the grace and ease of a *Swan Lake* ballerina. Tunes like "Walk on By," "Soulful Strut," and "Baby Elephant Walk" are accompanied by quick color changes, set to go with the flow of the music's timbre and tempo.

When the fountain first sprouted in 1962, as the brainchild of eighteen volunteers—many of whom continue in the operations today—it was clearly the world's largest musical fountain. Leave it to Las Vegas to recently take that title away from a town with 11,168 residents. But Grand Haven's not one to rest on its laurels. Thirty new productions were added in 1997, a costly and labor-intensive project. Totally automated, one minute of water formations requires one hour of programming.

During the daylight, it's difficult to decipher the fountain's presence on Dewey Hill, even though it's the size of a football field. It doesn't look like much of anything when it's not making music.

But for more than forty years it's had an untarnished record of operation . . . that is, until May 2002, when a computer glitch caused the first show stoppage in history.

At the end of each performance, landlubbers applaud and the boats in the harbor honk in appreciation and all head either home or to one of the outdoor cafes, trying to piece together the puzzle of why a man would be talking in the fountain in the first place. Seems like woman's work to me.

The Musical Fountain performs every night at dusk from Memorial Day until Labor Day.

Find the intersection of Harbor and Washington and you'll be about as close as you can get. Donations are accepted. For more information or special requests, call Jim Bonamy at (616) 847–4894.

## SQUARE VERSION OF THE OVAL OFFICE
### Grand Rapids

The first voice you hear is that of Marvin Gaye questioning through his poignant lyrics, "What's Going On?" Your words precisely. Isn't this the Gerald R. Ford Museum, paying tribute to our country's thirty-eighth President? Nothing very presidential among the Janis Joplin and Jimi Hendrix posters or the Disco Fever dance floor with flashing colored lights. You soon realize, however, this is a 1970s overview, enabling you to become totally immersed into the sights and

*The nation's first exact replica of the Oval Office exposes itself for public viewings in Grand Rapids.*

sounds of the era in which Grand Rapids' favorite son led the nation.

From here, you'll go through 41,000 square feet of galleries exhibiting every phase of Ford's life through attention-getting high-tech multimedia presentations. Among the expected displays, such as christening gowns and gifts to the nation, are remembrances Ford himself may want to forget: tools used in the Watergate break-in and the gun Squeaky Fromme used in her assassination attempt.

In the past, getting inside the Oval Office off-hours may have been an opportunity afforded only to White House interns. Here, anyone is welcome in the first exact replica, with its stately measurements of 35 by 29 by 18 ½ feet, the latter being the ceiling height. A six-minute illuminated audio presentation, rated G and dedicated to Bob and Dolores Hope, recreates a typical day during Ford's tenure, quite different from the hypothetical X-rated version of Bill Clinton's.

Former president Ford has the final say on everything that goes into this impressive structure and pays personal visits four or five times a year. Every president since Herbert Hoover has been the recipient of his own museum and library, although Ford's is the only facility that's split. His library sits miles away in Ann Arbor on the campus of his alma mater, the University of Michigan.

Attractively situated on the west bank of the Grand River in the heart of downtown at 303 Pearl Street Northwest, the Gerald R. Ford Museum is open 9:00 A.M. to 5:00 P.M. every day except New Year's Day, Thanksgiving, and Christmas. Admission charge. Call (616) 451–9263.

# PRESIDENT AND VICE PRESIDENT WITHOUT ONE VOTE

*M*ichigan is the home of the only person to become president of the United States without ever being elected either president or vice president. Gerald Ford of Grand Rapids was appointed vice president on December 6, 1973, when Spiro Agnew resigned the position after pleading no contest to income tax evasion.

The next year, on August 9, 1974, Ford took the oath of office of the president, replacing Richard Nixon who left the White House over the Watergate scandal.

## *ACCORDIONISTS SQUEEZE MORE OUT OF LIFE*
### *Grand Rapids*

A t first Kay Tomaszewski may not appear to be the most likely candidate to serve as mistress of ceremonies, secretary, and general goodwill ambassador for the Grand Rapids Accordion Ensemble, the largest independent group of accordionists in the country, because she herself has never pushed a single key on the squeeze box.

You see, her husband, Ray, was an accordion-playing aficionado—the proud owner of sixteen of 'em—who in 1991 gathered a group of Lawrence Welk wannabes together for the purpose of practicing, performing, and, frankly, bringing some Aretha-style R-E-S-P-E-C-T to the oft-maligned instrument. The next year Ray passed away, but his memory lives on through the music that the now forty-five-member-strong association shares with audiences all over the state.

Each week, under the direction of Dominic Marinelli, of "Dominic and the Dominoes" fame, men and women ages thirty-something to seventy-something rehearse diligently for hours to perfect their 125-tune repertoire, ranging from "New York, New York" to "Itsy-Bitsy-Teeny-Weenie Yellow Polka-Dot Bikini" to their rabble-rousing finale, "Beer Barrel Polka." Thrown into the mix for good measure are "some romantic numbers that would just knock your eyeballs out." (Now that's romantic imagery.)

Never missing a practice or concert, Kay additionally displays her accordion affection in her home, where more than 500 figurines garnered since 1948—each with instrument in hand—line ceiling-height shelves. (Help is called in for dusting duty.) It came as no surprise that, when the prestigious VanAndel Museum recently held a contest to honor exceptional hobby-

*Kay Tomaszewski in her "accordion room," putting the squeeze on Ivan, her prized accordionist from Russia.*

ists, Kay beat out the competition to earn her own place in museum history.

If you're interested in bringing your accordion out of the closet or to check on concert schedules for the Grand Rapids Accordion Ensemble, contact their Web site at www.1serv.net/ ~rwhit.com.

## DA HORSE DA VINCI DA SIGNED
### Grand Rapids

**M**ilan—Grand Rapids—Milan. It's a trip that took 500 years for Leonardo da Vinci's horse to complete. Today the world's largest bronze horse sculpture has taken up permanent residence in the Frederik J. Meijer Gardens and Sculpture Park, while its identical twin is an Italian citizen.

A little background will help . . . In 1482 da Vinci was commissioned by the duke of Milan to create the grandest equine statue ever known. A big assignment, resulting in twenty-five years of work. (Cut him some slack; he had other projects, like completing *The Last Supper*.) Finishing touches had just been put on the three-story-high clay model when war broke out, and the French invaders found great pleasure in using it for target practice. The creative genius died in 1519, lamenting on his deathbed the loss of his cherished steed.

That would have been the end of the story, but in 1967 da Vinci's thumbnail sketches of the horse miraculously reappeared. To see the project through to the end became the mission of pilot and part-time sculptor Charles Dent, but then he, too, died, and many thought the animal was jinxed.

An article in the *New York Times* prompted Fred Meijer to step in, vowing to do whatever he could to make da Vinci's dream come true. The third time was the charm, with artist Nina Akamu supplying the interpretation that resulted in the 24-foot-high, fifteen-ton, Renaissance-style *American Horse*. Out of the same mold, now broken, came the *Italian Horse*, standing in Milan, Italy.

Visitors from Italy come to Grand Rapids, and vice versa, to try to detect the subtlest of differences, of which there are none. Except the Italian stallion, on its marble pedestal, stands 6 feet closer to heaven than the American in the courtyard of

*Put out to pasture for more than five centuries, da Vinci's horse
now strikes a statuesque pose in Meijer Gardens.*

the Meijer Gardens, accessible for a "mind-expanding" touchy-feely experience. Do you think perhaps they're receiving vibes from da Vinci signaling approval of his now completed work?

The Frederik Meijer Gardens and Sculpture Park is found at 1000 East Beltline Northeast. It's open Monday through Saturday 9:00 A.M. to 5:00 P.M., Sunday noon to 5:00 P.M., 363 days a year; closed Christmas and New Year's. Get in touch with them at (616) 957–1580 or (888) 957–1580, or on their Web site www.meijergardens.org.

Admission charge for adults and children five years and older.

# TULIPS BEHEADED FOR TWO LIPS

*I*n Holland, Michigan, tulips are not to be taken lightly. As a matter of fact, they're not to be taken at all. If for some odd reason you feel the sudden urge to run up and pick one of the 6 million that blossom each spring, it's a $100 fine.

In May 1998 Eric Balcazar found out the hard way that the city is serious about the penalty. Just before Tulip Time—the third largest flower show in North America, drawing more than a million people—the twenty-year-old was accused of beheading not just one, but as many as 2,000 tulips.

Love may be blind, but a photographer wasn't. During Eric's trial a picture showed up in court of his girlfriend, smiling broadly, with none other than a tulip clenched between her teeth. Admitting that he clipped the 'lips (but only 975 of them) to impress her, his unlawful expression of affection cost him $740 in restitution, twenty-five days in jail, and eighty hours of community service.

Holland District Judge Hannes Meyers Jr. divided the sentence: fifteen days behind bars immediately, the remaining ten during the next year's Tulip Time. Hoping that the hours of community service would be spent planting bulbs for the city, Judge Meyers also issued an official advisory: From now on, "tiptoe through town very carefully."

# S A L V A G I N G   A R T
## *H o l l a n d*

A s soon as I saw the canine Q-tip bouncing toward me, I knew that Padnos Iron and Metal Company in Holland wasn't your run-of-the-mill scrap-iron recycling center.

The expression *meaner than a junkyard dog* doesn't apply to Shavov, the barely 10-pound bichon frise who guards the office of CEO Louis Padnos. But it takes more than a cute dog to make the cover of *Scrap Iron Magazine*, the "Voice of the Recycling Industry." About ten years ago Louis started turning designs created by his artist wife into scrap-iron sculptures that are seen around Holland and ring the thirty-five acres of the metal recycling facility.

When Louis's father began the scrap-iron business in 1905, he probably had no idea that someday his "junkyard" would become a tourist attraction. The first piece he did was just a bent piece of pipe that he thought would make an interesting flagpole. He showed it to his wife, Karen, who encouraged him to use his imagination and see what happened.

What happened led to the first decorative sculptures around the property. Before you could say *iron-art*, people were getting interested.

One of the people who expressed an interest was Frederick Meijer, who built Meijer Gardens in Grand Rapids where such prestigious works as the giant horse *El Cavallo*, based on the plans of Leonardo da Vinci, stands. Meijer invited Padnos to display several of his pieces at Meijer Gardens for an entire summer, and now four pieces are part of the permanent collection.

The artwork runs the gamut from abstract to whimsical figures that portray a 21-foot marching band figure in front of the main admissions building at Grand Valley State University.

"My wife and I have been art collectors for many years," says Patnos. "To classify myself as a serious artist . . ." His voice modestly trails off.

"I take the attitude that I know it's not great art but if it brings a smile to people's faces as they go by, then it's done its job and I've done mine."

Louis has a file full of letters from people writing to tell him that he has done just that. It's those letters that help him counter the doubters. "When people look at the scrap business and call it a blight, I keep telling them that beauty is in the eyes of the beholder." What he has tried to do with scrap metal is give them an eyeful.

The Padnos Iron and Metal Company is located at 195 West Eighth Street; (616) 396–6521. Open Monday through Friday 7:00 A.M. to 5:00 P.M.

## PADDLE POPS
### Holland

No matter where I go in Michigan, it seems every town has some kind of food that locals insist I have to try before my visit is complete. Such was the case regarding the Holland, Michigan, paddle pop. And the place to pick a paddle pop is the Holland Peanut Store. Investigative journalist that I am, I had to comply.

Although they've been doing business at their current location since 1954, the Fabiano family has been in the chocolate business since 1902. And they're still making goodies in a family way. It seems everybody in the store is a brother, sister, aunt, or uncle. Now, you'd think that a family that is a chocoholic's Valhalla would have members approximately the size of one of the windmills that dot the area, but that's not the case.

Mary (Fabiano) Stille, one of the sisters who helps run the business, says the answer is moderation. Moderation may be the family's motto, but it doesn't seem to apply to the customers. Apparently it's not uncommon for people to walk out with more than $100 worth of goodies. "If they didn't, we wouldn't be here," chirps the barely-a-size-2 Mary.

The store also does corporate orders for gift baskets and jars of assorted nuts, which make up a big piece of the business, but it's the individual sweet tooth that carries the brunt of the load.

You're probably thinking, "It's great reading about a family-owned business that's been around all that time, but what about the paddle pops?"

There's a method to my madness. If I'd told you about paddle pops in the first paragraph, your mouth would've started watering, and chances are you'd need a chocolate "fix" more than you'd need to know about the Fabiano family and their Dutch treats. It's kind of like making you eat all your vegetables before you have your dessert. But you've read this far, so here goes.

A paddle pop is a huge slice of ice cream with a "paddle" stuck in the end. It's then dipped in homemade chocolate, not once but twice; but the real secret of paddle pop perfection is the way the chopped peanuts are lovingly roasted before they are wrapped around the chocolate-covered confection.

Is ice cream on a stick alone worth a drive to Holland? Absolutely not. That's why I recommend you justify it by buying about a dozen paddle pops to take home and stick in the freezer. Think of it as doing your part to conserve our precious fossil fuels.

The Holland Peanut Store is at 46 East Eighth Street; call (616) 392–4522. Open Monday, Thursday, and Friday 9:30 A.M. to 9:00 P.M.; Tuesday, Wednesday, and Saturday 9:30 A.M. to 5:30 P.M. Closed Sunday.

# CLOMPING TO THE BEAT

*I*'ve always had tremendous respect for members of marching bands. Playing an instrument is tough enough, but doing it while you're marching in time and trying to form a giant kumquat in a "Salute to Salads" boggles my mind.

The Holland High School Marching Dutchman Band, however, not only plays, marches, and makes formations, but also does it in unforgiving wooden shoes. Walking in wooden shoes is tough enough; marching in them should require a purple heart from Dr. Scholl.

It turns out the secret of marching in wooden shoes is "socking it to them." The 150 band members wear, on the average, about four pair of thick wool socks under the wooden shoes that they purchase at Holland's Dutch Village. Although Dutch dancers in Dutch costumes carrying the Netherlands' flags have replaced the traditional majorettes, both drum majors do their high-stepping in their lumber loafers.

Band director Charles Boulard, who has been directing the band since 1980, isn't Dutch but does wear wooden shoes. During his tenure, he's shepherded his wooden-shod flock to the 1985 presidential inaugural parade, the 1995 Tournament of Roses parade, the January 1, 1998, Disney World Main Street parade, and every year in the Holland TulipTime Parades, playing—what else?—"Tiptoe through the Tulips."

## COUGARS AND TIGERS AND BEARS, OH MY—YES, AND THEY REALLY DO ALL FLY!
### Kalamazoo

A zoo where cobras and camels fly? It really does exist. It's the Kalamazoo Air Zoo, a 100,000-square-foot hangar packed with more than seventy of the world's most remarkable aircraft. These were the wings that played a major role in our country's preservation of peace in World War II, the Vietnam War, and more recently the Persian Gulf War.

The "zoo" fulfills the dreams of Pete and Sue Parish, both pilots who served in World War II. Opened in 1979, their menagerie includes a Wildcat, Bearcat, Hellcat, Tigercat, and Ms. Parish's own Curtiss Warhawk P-40. It's this aviation wonder that stands out with its pink (make that *desert pink*) exterior and painted trimmings of lipstick, eye shadow, and the longest lashes this side of Betty Boop. A one-seater, it has an assigned crew weight of 120 pounds, perfect for Parish, who at age eighty continues to fly her own plane.

If you want to experience flight firsthand, for an additional charge you can go up in the first commercial airliner, a Ford trimotor. It's one of only four remaining in the world today.

It's hard to miss the 48-by-14-foot wall mural titled *Between a Rock and a Hard Place.* Kalamazoo artist Richard Herter has created a masterpiece here. No, your eyes aren't playing tricks on you. He designed it so that no matter where you stand, that B-17 bomber is always coming toward you.

The Kalamazoo Air Museum is also home to the Michigan Aviation Hall of Fame and the Guadalcanal Memorial Museum. Visit them at 3101 East Milham. An admission fee is charged. The hours June through August are Monday through Saturday 9:00 A.M. to 6:00 P.M., Sunday noon to 6:00 P.M.; the rest of the year it closes at 5:00 P.M. Contact (269) 382–6555 or www.airzoo.org.

### ROLLER COASTER IN A SANDBOX?
### IT CAN BE DUNE!
#### Mears

The afternoon began with a search for fulgurites. Mind you, with no idea what a fulgurite was, much less what it looked like, this wasn't an easy task. But the Silver Lakes Sand Dunes Area is one of the few places in the country where they're common.

Checking in with Jack Warfield, owner of Sandy Korners Jeep Rentals, I unearthed the mystery of the fulgurite. It's formed when lightning strikes sand, fusing into linear structures resembling seagull droppings. Warfield, who's been "playing dune buggy" for thirty years, has never found one himself, although some are on hand so you know what you're "preying" for.

Our first stop was Proctologist Point, where the "doctor" examines the emissions of all vehicles entering the state park by inserting a rod into the exhaust system. Ouch!

We then head down a sandy, bumpy path toward a parking lot filled with dirt bikes, jeeps, dune buggies, trucks with bumper barbeque grills . . . anything that goes off-road, all assembled reminiscent of a college tailgate party. Approaching Mount Baldie, a 200-foot heap of sand, it's mind-boggling to hear that twice a year nearly a hundred vehicles race up its face in a heart-stopping 1.9 seconds.

Ladies and gentlemen, it's now time to rev your stomachs for the ride of your life, or else they'll be revved up for you. To the apex of the first dune mountain we go, where the view is captivating, if not a bit alarming: the majesty of Lake Michigan on one side, the serenity of Silver Lake on the other. Then it's up and down, straight down, over and over again at a pace something less than the 90 mph of those zipping by. Each peak brings another surprise in this sanctuary of 500 acres of sand. Granted, you hear the *vroom, vroom* of other engines; you're still in a world of your own. Occasionally I shake my head in disbelief as vehicles stop at the top, appearing to be teetering on the edge. If someone inside should shift his weight the teeniest bit . . . oops!

We stop, too, as Jack sets up an impromptu drag race by dropping the mandatory 10-foot-long, international orange flag on the front of his buggy. In a matter of seconds, a dozen vehicles line up, the flag flips up, and the chase is on without a word ever spoken.

My hour regretfully is over. Did I find any fulgurites? What fulgurites? I knew I'd forgotten something.

Silver Lake Sand Dunes is unique in that it's the only dune east of Utah on which you can ride your own vehicle. Sandy Korners, at 1762 North 24th Avenue in Mears, rents four-person buggies you drive yourself—$85 an hour per vehicle—rain or shine, every day May through October. For reservations, call (231) 873–5048 or find them on the Web at www.sandykorners.com.

## WHITE SAILS IN THE SAWDUST
### Montague

O ne of the weather vane commandments declares, "Thou shalt have 1 inch of weather vane height for every one foot of roofline." At 48 feet tall, the world's largest weather vane needs a roof the size of the Mackinac Bridge.

Instead, the hand-formed aluminum breeze barometer, created by Whitehall Products—which just happens to make more weather vanes than anyone else—found a home on the corner of Dowling and Water Streets, its second residence. The first was a sawdust-filled peninsula—the result of the lumbering era—where the 4,300-pound structure stood or tried to stand for fifteen years. Not pulp fiction, the weather vane, with its 11-foot-tall ship topper, was sinking in the sawdust. Its only chance for survival was to be landlocked.

Speaking of sinking ships, that's exactly what the crowning glory of the vane represents: the Great Lakes lumber schooner *Ella Ellenwood*. Home-based on nearby White Lake, the *Ellenwood* ran aground 8 miles north of Milwaukee during a perilous storm in the fall of 1901. The crew abandoned ship, but the blustery winds blew the ship apart, leaving no remnants until the next spring, when a section of the ship's nameplate, bearing the word ELLENWOOD, was found in White Lake. By the grace of Neptune, it had drifted all the way across Lake Michigan, returning to the exact spot it had taken off from. Who says you can never go home again?

You can verify the nameplate's existence at Montague City Hall, where it's permanently displayed.

The fully operational weather vane, at last check, was standing in town, and on extremely windy days has the ship doing 360s faster than an exorcised head. All weather-related and unrelated questions can be answered by contacting the White Lake Area Chamber of Commerce at (231) 893–4585, (800) 879–9702, or www.whitelake.org.

## *S U B   P E R F O R M S   M U L T I P L E   L I F E - S A V I N G   O P E R A T I O N S*
### *M u s k e g o n*

The rising-sun decals on the bridge silently speak volumes. Thirty Japanese ships sunk; fourteen others damaged. The record of the USS *Silversides,* now sitting in Muskegon's Pere

Marquette Park, gives it the distinction of being the most successful surviving wartime submarine.

The "Lucky Boat" appeared to have been blessed from early on. In December 1943 George Platter, fireman second class, watched as his personal bombshell fell, a gangrenous appendix in need of immediate removal. What do you do in the middle of the ocean with no one on board who's ever performed an operation? That's when Pharmacist Mate Thomas More stepped in, with galley knife in hand, executing his first appendectomy on the officers' dining table. Six days later, after toppling out of his rigged-up bunk during a death charge, Platter returned to active duty. The account lives as perhaps the most celebrated seafaring surgery of all time.

As you walk the 312-foot distance through half a dozen entries no bigger than 18 by 30 inches, a tour of the *Silversides* enables history to come alive. Anecdotes galore provided by your guide will keep all ages entertained. Like the story of the captain's dog, Admiral, who made it through four months at sea—albeit illegally—to return home in need of a little fire hydrant education.

Torpedo Man Third Class Mike Harbin was the only man to die on board—on May 10, 1942, hit by enemy fire. Unsubstantiated reports of haunting noises and furnishings that have mysteriously moved suggest that Harbin's ghost remains lodged inside.

You can check all this and more out for yourself by spending the night on board *Silversides*. There's room for seventy-two guests in four cramped quarters. (You'll get to know your neighbor *really* well.) Two other ships, a Coast Guard cutter and an LST, accommodate another eighty-eight. Guests are mostly youth-oriented groups, but anyone is welcome. Book early . . . there's up to a year's wait for weekends. Weekday rates run $17; weekends, $21.

The Great Lakes Naval Memorial Museum, including the USS *Silversides,* is open April through October. Times vary for the hour-long tours, and a fee is charged. Call (231) 755–1230 or log onto www.silversides.org.

## THE NOT-SO-SECRET GARDEN
### Muskegon

Take dirt. Add flowers, a walking bridge, and archways. Mix together with countless hours of research and back-breaking bulb planting. Watch it rise into Monet's Giverny Garden in Muskegon.

The recipe belongs to Master Gardener and local businesswoman Florence Bright, whose vision and commitment transformed a vacant 65-by-74-foot city lot into an authentic replica of Monet's garden, right down to the exact shades of water lilies in the pond.

*Monet's brush strokes a downtown Muskegon lot*
*duplicating his Giverny Garden.*

Pulling together the talents of horticulturists at the Michigan State Extension and Master Gardener volunteers, the vigorous work began. Obstacles inevitably cropped up. Topsoil brought in was so hard you needed a jackhammer to dig into it. A water line was accidentally cut, providing instant irrigation. All worth it when the end result blossomed the following year.

Now, as you cross the crushed pink concrete walkways—yes, Monet had those, too—you'll find a pocket park filled with arbors of roses, dahlias, geraniums, peonies, and the necessary climatic adjustment of icicle pansies. Japanese maples and a (dwarf) weeping willow complete the breathtaking duplication.

It's a living palate, as the artist would have said, occasionally bringing lives together permanently as couples say "I do" under the arches.

Save yourself the trip to France by visiting the corner of Clay and Fifth in historic downtown Muskegon. The gardens are in bloom from April until the first frost. For more information, call the MSU Extension at (231) 724–6361.

## ONE MAN'S JUNK MAIL IS ANOTHER MAN'S FORTUNE

*Indirectly you can blame Niles, Michigan, for all those catalogs crowding your mailbox. Perhaps if eleven-year-old Aaron Montgomery Ward had been happier here while earning 25 cents a day working in a local barrel factory, he might never have been inclined to start the country's first mail-order business. In 1872 he sent out a single page offering 162 items for sale with a "satisfaction or money-back" guarantee. When he died forty-one years later, Montgomery Ward had annual sales of $40 million.*

### *A*ND *THE W*IENER *IS* . . .
#### *Rockford*

**W**here can you go for four hours of work and be inducted into a hall of fame? Try starting out at the corner bar. Not just any corner bar, but the one and only Corner Bar, the oldest building in the town of Rockford, where people put their stomachs on the table for a chance to be inducted into the Hot Dog Hall of Fame.

The rules for membership are simple: Eat twelve hot dogs with at least the special chili sauce, developed by a former army cook at Prohibition's end, in one four-hour sitting and you're a wiener! Your name goes up on the wall alongside the other 5,000 in the fellowship. Extra credit can be earned by consuming twenty or more—then the dogs and an official congratulatory T-shirt are on the house.

Originated in 1965, people from all over the world have gone into the "hall" with the grand championship awarded on March 15, 1982, to Sharon Scholten of Kentwood, Michigan, who surpassed the eight-year record by consuming, within the allotted time frame, forty-two and a half of the Corner Bar coneys. That extra half that put her over the top. If it sounds too "inedible" to believe, a copy of the *Grand Rapids Press* article featuring Scholten's victory photo can be seen in the entrance and on the cover of the menu.

Words of advice for potential applicants who are thinking of mustering up the courage to catch up on the record: Eat something small beforehand so your stomach is in the expansion mode, and make sure you bring enough cash. One young man recently was pumped up after devouring a dozen in two and a half hours, only to be deflated when he discovered he couldn't pay his bill, forcing him to chow down another eight so his total consumption would be complimentary.

*If they were foot-longs, they'd have served
7,249,440. With shorter dogs, the number stands
much higher.*

The chili dogs are $1.30 a piece; the fat-free version tacks on another 40 cents. Even if you don't succeed, you can buy a hall of fame T-shirt. Your friends back home won't know the difference. The Corner Bar with its novel take-out window is on the corner at 31 North Main Street. Open Monday through Thursday 11:00 A.M. to 10:00 P.M., Friday and Saturday 11:00 A.M. to 11:00 P.M., Sunday noon to 8:00 P.M. Call (616) 866–9866.

*FORMICA, NEON, AND A BASKET OF FRIES*
*Rockford*

*D*iner: (Dye-ner, n.) A restaurant in the shape of a railroad dining car.

Throwbacks to the 1940s, most diners are long gone now, yet oddly enough you can find of a trio of the neon flashers sitting on M57 in Rockford. What Diana Ross did for the Supremes, Rosie's is doing for Dinerland: holding everyone together while getting ready to branch off to stardom on her own.

Baby boomers may well remember Rosie's diner for the Bounty paper towels commercials featuring Nancy Walker as Rosie the waitress. Well, this is the authentic "quicker picker-upper car" where all those spots were filmed, now plunked between two other oldies, but goodies, just like her, only not as famous.

Purchased by artist Jerry Berta in Little Ferry, New Jersey, and transported in two sections—"four days, ten flat tires, and one fire"—Rosie arrived safely in Rockford. An instant success in 1991, only five years later she honored her one-millionth customer.

Time has taken its toll on Rosie; and even though she's still open for business, her once glistening stainless exterior looks a little worn. Her two sidekicks never did much on their own. One houses a rarely open gift shop; the other has "plans" in the works. And the quirky miniature golf out back with hot dog and hamburger sculptures? Also on the agenda for renovation.

Under new ownership in '02, let's hope the hula-hoop onion rings keep gliding across the Formica while we hear Rosie's jukebox blasting Gloria Gaynor's "I Will Survive."

Rosie's is located on 4500 14 Mile Road (M57). Open Monday through Thursday 6:00 A.M. to 8:00 P.M., Friday and Saturday 6:00 A.M. to 9:00 P.M., Sunday 7:00 A.M. to 8:00 P.M. Call (616) 866–FOOD or (616) 866–ARTS.

## *A BRASSY BASH? SEND IN THE CLOWNS*
### *Scottville*

Here they come, just a stumblin' down the street, playing a down 'n' dirty, bump 'n' grind version of "The Stripper." These are the men of the Scottville Clown Band, 200 members strong, with wailing trumpets and clarinets blasting out blues that would stop a crowd from drinking on Bourbon Street.

It's been that way since 1903, when musical merchants dressed down in their weekend worst to entertain customers. A wide cross section of professions fills today's roster: doctors, teachers, truck drivers, school band directors, a judge, and a blacksmith are among those packing up their instruments and heading to Scottville, dubbed the "Clown Town," for seventeen rehearsals a year. Each a superbly accomplished musician, the end result is hundreds of performance requests and skyrocketing sales of CDs.

Led by a hobo in blackface with a toilet plunger for a baton, the "bums" take their penchant for fun as seriously as they do their music. Individualized band uniforms range from the ridiculous to the sublime . . . one wears a tutu and tights with a C-clamp for an earring; another is a Miss Piggy look-alike. And occasionally "groupies" will filter through bearing signs, WILL U MARRY ME?

The bonds of friendship and camaraderie provide impetus while the serious side of their nonprofit organization raises funds for musical scholarships statewide. All costume, travel, and general expenses are paid out of each member's personal resources, making the convivial clowning "a very expensive hobby," worth every penny.

Their annual "world tour," comprised of fifty play dates, doesn't always result in their typical post at the rear end of the parade. Often in demand is their "clean socks and shorts

*Miss Piggy, aka Fred G. Lyons, marches to his/her own
beat, hoping not to lose an eyelash.*

concert," categorically a far more formal affair with a sit-down
audience and maybe a bow tie or two sprucing up the baggy
pants, hula skirts, and silly hats with arrows shooting through
their heads.

It tickles the heart to know that a hundred years hasn't
changed one thing . . . the sound of laughter from the crowd is
always music to these bozos' ears.

The best place to get all the scoop is either from their Web
site at www.scottvilleclownband.com or through the
secretary/drum major George Wilson, (231) 757–2227.

## A Gem of a Friend to Men
*Shelby*

**T**he idyllic backdrop for a fairy tale, crystal-clear gems the size of pearl onions adorn the state's royalty: Miss Michigan, the Cherry Queen, Mrs. Asparagus. Surprise, it's only make-believe. Not the royalty part. The jewels; they're fake. The manufactured product of the Shelby Gem Factory.

Winding through streets in the small town of Shelby, at the end of a lonely industrial parkway, you hardly expect to find such authentic-looking "rocks" engineered inside the rather nondescript-looking building.

The birthplace of more gemstone products than anywhere else in the world was conceived in 1970 by Larry Kelly, who grew up next door in Hart and didn't see any reason to leave. After all, the necessary chemicals are shipped in from the four corners of the earth, and you really don't need to inspect the gems in person to make a purchase. If you see one diamond, you've seen them all, each an exact clone of the next, varying only in shape and size. Same goes for the rubies, emeralds, and sapphires that come off the assembly line.

The secrets of Hollywood stars—rumored to be more than a few—remain hidden inside; company policy forbids disclosure of the names of anyone who has opted for a "falsie."

Some odd requests have been made over the years—like the woman who had bone removed from her foot, then requested the knucklebone be set with a "Shelby gem" to be worn as an anklet. A retired plumber in search of that special "drip" coming down from his golden faucet found it in a pear-shaped diamond. The record, though, goes to the man who bought the biggest multifaceted stone ever custom-created—a forty-carat insert for the center of his steering wheel.

*At 50 carats, even Elizabeth Taylor would require
more than one finger to hold this ring upright.*

The insurance industry put the kibosh on their factory
tours, but the theater runs a video of the whole process. A
hands-on faceting machine gives everyone the chance to experience the grunt and grind of the gemcutter's life.

At $130 a carat, regardless of shape, these diamonds in the
rough could just be a guy's best friend.

Shelby Man Made Gemstones is located at 1330 Industrial
Drive; (231) 861–2165. It's open Monday through Friday 9:00
A.M. to 5:30 P.M., Saturday noon to 4:00 P.M.

# FINALLY, A HOTEL THAT'S RIGHT ON TRACK

## South Haven

O nly *really* big news makes the front page two days in a row. The arrival of not one, but two raging red cabooses in South Haven met that criterion for the local newspaper some twenty years ago.

What began as an innocent southern Illinois business trip for Bob Burr ended up in the purchase of "a little something" to bring home to his wife, Pat—a pair of tail-end train cars. (She might have been just as happy with a four-slice toaster.) Fanfare and hoopla never seen before in this resort community greeted the newcomers' arrival at their humble abode on the site of the out-of-service train depot.

And there they sat on abandoned tracks until people started asking "if their kids could spend the night." Before too long, grown-up kids wanted to rest their head on a piece of railroad history, too. So the Burrs renovated both interiors (leaving the privacy of the conductor's loft intact), added screen porches, and baptized them "The Caboose Hotel."

Train buffs and those who simply favor "detachment" start dialing on April Fool's Day to put in their reservations. By the first of May, both cars generally are filled for the next five months. Pat, who spends her days with a mop and Lysol in hand to keep the "twins" spotless, may be the only person who can't wait to see the autumnal equinox. That's when both she and the rails shut down until the following spring.

Open April though October, the hotel's rates in 2002 were $104.00 for double occupancy, $5.00 per person beyond that. The air-conditioned cabooses sit on the tracks at 162 Dunkley Avenue. Directly across the street is the Burr's latest acquisition, the former coal station, also available for nightly rentals. To reserve a spot in either location, call (269) 637–6276.

Beaver
Island

Petoskey ⑶¹

Charlevoix Horton Bay
⑬¹
Ironton

⑹⁶
Northport Eastport

Suttons Bay ⑻⁸
⑶¹
⑵²
⑵² Acme
Traverse ⑺² Kalkaska
City
⑶⁷ ⑬¹

⑵²
Putney
Corners ⑶¹
⑴¹⁵
Kaleva ⑸⁵

⑸⁵ Cadillac
⑶⁷
⑬¹

⑴¹⁵ ⑴²⁷
⑴⁰

⑴²⁷

# PINKIE PLAYGROUND

# PINKIE
# PLAYGROUND

O riginally this chapter was titled "Frozen Cherries," but it was modified partially to remain in keeping with the symbolic image of the shape of the hand, and also so as not to rock the tractor of the vast number of cherry farmers in southwest Michigan. How prophetic that alteration proved to be. The '02 cherry crop bit the ice so often that replacements had to be flown in from out of state for July's National Cherry Festival in Traverse City.

So "Pinkie Playground" will hold. There's no disputing this area knows how to have fun 365 days a year, no matter what the weather. With the best snow skiing in the Lower Peninsula joining sunbaked shores of crystal-clear lakes, put two of anything on your feet or arms and it's "instant party." Venture out to the sandbar on Torch Lake and you'll see a conglomeration of two-legged and four-legged species hankering for a knee-deep walk on water. Or sail away to new heights in the state's only hang gliding near Frankfort.

Party animals are ubiquitous with a moose that slops kisses in a local tavern, an island that's gone to the birds, another dedicated to beavers, a whopper of a fish story, a cow that's been pinched and pulled in every direction, and an 18-foot grasshopper a wee bit too stiff for the bar-hopping scene.

And in this chapter I'll take the wraps off the secretive whereabouts of the preeminent tourist value: totally free and guaranteed to humor the stuffiest curiosity seeker.

*P U T   A N O T H E R   N I C K E L   I N*
*T H E   N I C K E L O D E O N*
*A c m e*

n 1904 the only sounds you heard from the building were *moo.* Today the site of this former 180-acre dairy farm echoes with the sounds of hundreds of mechanical instruments. It's heaven for those who may not have taken their piano lessons seriously, since all the instruments play by themselves.

The Music House Museum opened its doors to the public in 1983. Founded by five private collectors who recognized that only 3 percent of all mechanical instruments still exist, it now is home to items from more than 200 individuals.

And what you'll hear through the corridors of the "barn" is musically inspiring. All instruments have been fine-tuned to work as they did years ago. You can literally drop a nickel in the 1917 Cremona piano nickelodeon and hear an authentic honky-tonk version of "Jingle Bells."

Time hasn't altered the sound generated by the incredible reproductive talents of a 1925 piano especially built for Detroit auto magnates Mr. and Mrs. Fredrick Fisher. Thanks to the magic in the perforated paper rolls, you'll enjoy a private concert by twenty-six-year-old George Gershwin playing "Rhapsody in Blue." Yes, it'll be exactly as he played it, note for note, with all of his personal artistic expression.

Long before there were DJs, there were dance organs, and one of the grandest of them all fills the museum's loft. The Amaryllis from the Victoria Palace Ballroom in Belgium was built in 1922 and has the same vigorous reverberation that it did during those Roaring Twenties.

Check out the world's largest music box, built by Regina, which plays discs that are a far cry from the CDs of today, measuring a whopping 27 inches in diameter.

*A lofty Amaryllis you never have to water, with a
30-foot carved façade and a musical repertoire
of 2,200 dance tunes.*

It's a stroll down memory lane with everything set in historically accurate vignettes. Gastronomical tastes may have changed some over the years, of course, as witnessed at the Hurry Back Saloon, where a sampling of the menu on the wall offers biscotti, fireballs, and beef jerky.

The Music House Museum is found at 7377 U.S. Highway 31 North. It's open Monday through Saturday 10:00 A.M. to 4:00 P.M., May 1 through October 31, as well as holiday weekends Thanksgiving through New Year's. Contact (231) 938–9300 or www.musichouse.org.

## BLOOMERS BUTCHER AMERICA'S ONLY KING
### Beaver Island

A remote island, 32 miles north of Charlevoix, improperly labeled Beaver Island (there are no beavers; a cartographer came up with the far-fetched idea that the island is shaped like one) is the backdrop for America's only kingdom. James Jesse Strang, an attorney who became self-appointed royalty—a redundancy in some eyes—founded a Mormon settlement here in 1847.

With a couple of thousand followers, he went about setting laws of the land best suited to his personal desires. A flamboyant personality with an eye for the ladies, worn out from disguising his polygamous wife as his "male" secretary, he issued the ruling that church elders must all have two simultaneous marriages. Not a popular edict with the women, especially his first wife, who packed her bags and headed to Wisconsin.

That didn't discourage Strang, who hastily acquired five wives and twelve offspring. Unhappy with long skirts on gals, bloomers (less material, more leg) became mandatory dress, with those found in noncompliance publicly taken to the whipping post. Well, that did it. The troops were riled enough to take action into their own hands and in 1856, two bloomer busters shot and killed the only man who would ever be king in America.

With only 550 permanent residents at the last census, 200 departing in winter, Beaver Island is home to more wildlife than anything else. A two-hour ferry ride from the mainland transports tourists to another world, a tranquil setting with 54 miles of beaches to stroll without a single pair of bloomers in sight.

Contact the Beaver Island Chamber of Commerce for information on accommodations and to learn more about the wild St. Patrick's Day celebration: (231) 448–2505.

# STRIKE ANY CHORD—NO TUNE-UP NEEDED

"*Timbre, more timbre, quick!*" *Words from Frank Young-man spoken to the logs and brake drums filling his backyard that have grown to be music to his ears. One night the self-described musical activist was dropping wood on the fire when he heard tunes popping from the pulp and the light-bulb went off. Why not create a garden of sound using nature's own as the instruments? Seemed so obvious, and it sure beat showing up somewhere as old drywall.*

*A teacher by trade, he approached a professor at Central Michigan for permission to do an independent study project with the "final" a concert in the forest. A stepladder of various-sized branches became a xylophone. Other twigs, hung clothesline-style, play the musical scale. As for the brake drums, they add dulcet tones unmatched by earthly creations. All instruments are left as they were innately tuned by that Goddess of Good Vibes somewhere in the sky.*

*Frank passed his exam with soaring sounds and continues to hold spontaneous jam sessions with fellow members of the "Log Rhythms," but all are welcome. No experience or training is necessary as long as you can get past the unusualness of the presentation and are willing to cast your musical inhibitions to the wind.*

*Cadillac has embraced its maestro of the woods, hiring him as artist in residence for their Michigan Community Part-nership Program. Expect soon to hear and see people of all ages marching to the beat of their own drummer.*

*The Sound Garden project will be expanding to the downtown area of Cadillac at the Clam River Greenway off Chestnut Street. For more information, contact the Chamber of Commerce, 222 Lake Street, (231) 775–9776, or access their Web site at www.cadillacmichigan.com/soundgarden.*

*Fred has plans to upgrade his own garden by sawing a bowling ball in half to serve as giant log caps. In his spare time he's a member of the Jive at 5 Swing Band.*

# THE NEVER-FREEZING STORY

*P*rocrastinator's Paradise . . . that's what an aquatic section of Cadillac could be called. If you need a sure bet excuse for avoidance, simply say you'll do it "when Lake Cadillac, Lake Mitchell, and their connecting canal all freeze over." It's not that this area's supersensitive to global warming; the point is that no matter how low the temperatures go, these three have never frozen over at the same time.

Back in the days of lumbering when "log on" meant a fallen tree made it to the barge, the Clam Lake Canal was built as a convenient passageway, and for as long as anyone can remember, early each November it turns to ice. No surprise there. About a month or so later the lakes on either side chill out, and that's when the unexplainable happens . . . the canal thaws. As hard as they may try, no one's been able to figure out why this trio just can't get in sync, but it's a fact that will easily fill in any blank moment at your next cocktail party or will prevent you from being sent away as "the weakest link."

## HOMES FROM THE STONE AGE
### Charlevoix

*T*hese cottages are so delightfully quaint, you fully expect to see Snow White waltz through the front doors with Sneezy, Dopey, and Sleepy trailing close behind. They're affectionately known as the mushroom houses, because that's what they

*Residents dish up the "fungus among us" in the mushroom homes.*

resemble with their curvy, slanting cedar shake roofs, irregular chimneys, and round stone walls. The Disney behind the scenes was Earl Young, a man as fascinating as the homes he designed.

Born in Mancelona, Michigan, in 1889, he moved to his beloved Charlevoix at age ten. Neither an architect nor a builder but for sixty years a licensed real estate broker, Earl was simply in love with rocks and wanted to share his enthusiasm with the rest of the world by designing imaginative homes, reflecting the beauty of the area.

In the 1930s his work incorporating the stones of Michigan into livable spaces began. Fieldstone, local quarry limestone, boulders, Onaway limestone, even red stone barged over from the Soo Locks—they're all represented.

A portion of the celebrated homes, including the backless half house, sit in a triangle on Clinton, Grant, and Park Avenue. Young, a diminutive man barely standing 5 feet tall, built the home at 306 Park for himself. It's scaled to his size, filling out only 800 square feet; word is that an average-sized adult isn't able to stand up straight in the four-legged bathtub.

The remainder of the unique and pricey "hobbit" homes (some have sold for upward of a million dollars) are in an area known as Boulder Park, near the Charlevoix hospital. They're a must-see trademark of northern Michigan. Maps for self-guided tours can be obtained from the Charlevoix Chamber of Commerce at 408 Bridge Street. Contact (231) 547–2101 or www.charlevoix.org. A precious few are available for weekly rentals . . . (231) 547–6480.

## MICHIGAN'S SHAPE PREHISTORICALLY PREDESTINED
### Charlevoix

**M**ichigan may have been mapped out long before any cartographer got involved. A nine-ton limestone boulder is the centerpiece of the fireplace in the main dining room at the Weathervane Restaurant. It's not just any large stone that's filling space, though. If you look closely, it's in the shape of the Lower Peninsula of Michigan, complete with highway markings. Yes, that does appear to be I–75 running through the middle and U.S. Highway 131 on the left, with M23 to the right.

The restaurant is another example of Earl Young's infatuation with stones. Once a gristmill, Young bought the place and began his conversion. He got rid of the top two floors and replaced them with a roofline patterned after a gull's wing. The exterior was faced with limestone and Onaway stone from the local quarry. Then he found his prized "mapping" boulder in 1954 while building roads in Charlevoix. Using a heavy-duty crane to lift it through the roof was itself a remarkable feat.

What may be even more astonishing is what Young placed it on: a meteorite weighing the same as the massive boulder, a whopping nine tons. It's mind-boggling to think that both are identical in weight, yet the meteorite is only a quarter of the keystone's size.

Stafford's Weathervane Restaurant is located at 106 Pine River Lane. In summer it's open Monday through Friday 11:00 A.M. to 10:00 P.M., Saturday until 10:30 P.M.; Sunday shutdown is at 9:30 P.M. Call for off-season hours: (231) 547–4311.

*Eighteen tons and what do you get? An imposing fireplace serving as a map of Michigan.*

## ACRES AWEIGH

*It was 1957 when Mary Lou Morse's thriving honeybee business saw its big plans for expansion fall through the cracks. While the Eastport Inn was being trucked across a frozen Torch Lake, horrified crowds watched as the ice gave way and the building took a nosedive. Miraculously the inn was recovered and remains alive and well today on the site of Brownwood Farms—makers of the yummiest cherry butter in northern Michigan.*

*Anyone who remembers the Brownwood Farms Restaurant in its heydays of the 1960s might want to check out old photos of the singing waitstaff known as the "Honey Bees," for one of the groups more recognizable alums, actress Christine Lahti.*

*Brownwood Acres is on U.S. Highway 31 at the north end of Torch Lake. Call toll-free (877) 591–3101 or (231) 599–3101. Open Monday through Friday 8:30 A.M. to 5:00 P.M., Saturday 10:00 A.M. to 5:00 P.M., Sunday noon to 5:00 P.M.*

### LET FREEDOM WRING
#### Horton Bay

How does a town with only nineteen permanent residents attract a crowd of more than 12,000 on the Fourth of July? By staging the wildest, wackiest parade you've ever seen.

The place is Horton Bay, a village so small that it was officially swallowed up by Boyne City in 1999. Yet it truly maintains its independence on Independence Day. The parade dates back to the 1920s. You can check out the original photos on the walls of the old General Store. But the madcap version got its start in the late 1970s when Bill Ohle, whose family nearly a century ago operated the town's Stroud and Ohle sawmill, decided to put new guidelines in place. He wanted the parade to be different with no commercial entries and just loads of satirical fun.

Each year a theme is designated, and hundreds of summer residents from nearby communities put on their thinking caps and homemade costumes and literally march to the beat of

Saturday Night Live *gets tough competition each Fourth of July from the political parodies in the Horton Bay Parade.*

their own mowers, as is the case with the renowned synchronized lawn mower marching band.

One year, instead of the grand marshal, an eighty-something-year-old woman dressed in the world's largest cotton ball served as the Grand Marshmallow.

Local stores quickly sell out of prized commodity toilet plungers for use as munitions for the Horton Bay militia or the Queen's royal scepter. Of course Her Ma Jest T rides high atop her toilet bowl throne, begging for money so the royal family won't be flushed from their residence. By parade's end, a flurry of coins have found their way to the float, tallying up to hundreds of dollars.

Author Ernest Hemingway spent his boyhood summers in Horton Bay. He must be proud the citizens remain united in their proclamation of liver tea and justice for all.

For more information for either participants or spectators, you can call the General Store at (231) 582-7827.

## 25 MILES IN THREE MINUTES OR LESS
### *Ironton*

Talk about a shortcut. The Ironton Ferry has been saving people miles of driving, either by car or by horse, since 1884. Lake Charlevoix is shaped just oddly enough so that to get from one side to the other you have to drive either 23 miles one way or 27 miles in the other direction. Or you can take the ferry to cross the 620 feet of water.

The current *Vessel Charlevoix,* the official title designated by the Coast Guard, has been sailing since 1926. It makes trips from 6:30 A.M. to 10:30 P.M. seven days a week, mid-April to Thanksgiving, weather permitting. There's no schedule. When someone shows up, the boat leaves. Captain Robert Curtis shuttles more than 71,000 cars a year on the "two-and-three-quarter- to three-minute" trip. He says on his best eight-hour day, he carried 435 cars. With a capacity of four cars, that's at least 109 crossings.

Totally self-supporting, the 50-foot ferry has managed to keep rates much the same as they've been for years. One slight exception: In 2002 the price of transporting a bike went from 50 cents to $1.00.

Over time the Ironton Ferry has had its share of the limelight. During the mid-1900s Captain Sam Alexander made it into "Ripley's Believe It or Not" for traveling 15,000 miles without ever being more than a quarter mile from his home.

The ferry is operated by the Charlevoix County Transportation Authority. Call (231) 547–7200.

## A HOME WORTH BOTTLING UP
### *Kaleva*

"**B**ottoms Out" was the commanding cry that Finnish immigrant John J. Makinen issued his troops in the early 1940s as they fastidiously lined up 60,000 glass bottles. Your first thought might be, "Not very effective armor." That's where you're wrong.

As owner of Northwestern Bottling Works, somehow he stumbled upon the insulating properties of the glass he was manufacturing. Taking to heart the old expression *People who live in glass houses shouldn't throw anything away,* the biggest recycling project Kaleva has ever seen started to take shape. He decided to build his own glass house, cutting off the tops of already defective bottles, cementing them with his own secret-recipe mortar, thereby creating the exterior four walls.

*The homeowner may have given up $6,000 of*
*bottle deposits for the ultimate in insulated*
*walls.*

Makinen died before he could move in, but it must have been
a happy home nevertheless. Says so right on the front, the
words are one of several artistic expressions bottled throughout.

The Bottle House became a museum in 1980, operated by
the Kaleva Historical Society. There's nothing special about the
interior, a standard three-bedroom home. But the artifacts are
entertaining, as is the commentary by society representatives.
President Brian Smith provided the missing piece to the puzzle
of the century . . . why we in the Midwest don't call them "soft
drinks" or "soda" like the rest of the country. It was the "pop"
of the cork out of Makinen's bottles that's never left us.

Other home-grown Kalevans include Ella and Lila Widgren, who went on to become nationally known as the Tony twins (you may remember those dreadful smelling home-permanent kits of the 1950s and 1960s) and Darth Vader, more familiar to some as the voice of CNN, James Earl Jones. Smith ends our tour by asking, "What would Ella Fitzgerald's new name be if she married Darth Vader?" Don't think too hard.

You can examine all the bottles with their raised lettering insignia KALEVA anytime at 14551 Wuoski Avenue at the corner of Kauko. There are limited hours to eye the inside: May through December Saturdays and Sundays only, noon to 4:00 P.M. Other times by appointment. Call (231) 362-2080.

*INSECT TO INSPECT . . . CLOSELY*
*Kaleva*

**W**hy is a grasshopper, 10 feet high, 18 feet long, weighing 500 pounds, standing guard at the Kaleva Centennial Walkway? In a roundabout way, to pay homage to the Finnish settlers' patron saint, St. Urho.

The Legend of the Farmer's Nightmare states that it was St. Urho, with his mighty pitchfork, who chased all the grasshoppers out of Finland, rescuing the vineyards from their throes of destruction. Truth be told, grapes don't grow in Finland. The story arrived here via Minnesota, and how trusting can you be of a state whose governor once said he wanted to be reincarnated as a bra?

But the myth served as impetus for Brethren High School Service Learning and Manistee Intermediate School students to create their own version of the giant crop killer, in exact proportions, out of 100 percent recycled metal. The big bug's nose in another life cooked someone's dinner as a Weber grill, its

*This artistically perfect grasshopper, known as the Farmer's
Nightmare, was built entirely by local students.*

legs are old railroad spikes, and the scales on its neck were
once shovel faces.

Under the direction of Wellston's Andy Priest, the project
has met with huge community appreciation. Dedicated on
March 16, 2000, the feast day of St. Urho, there's not been one
sign of grasshoppers infiltrating the area. My guess is, they're
attacking the vineyards of Minnesota at this very moment.

To see if any part of the grasshopper once belonged to you,
take Wuoski Avenue to Walta Street. Turn left, look right, and
you'll spot it. Project Kaleva is most helpful with any area
information. Call (231) 362–3480 or visit www.kalevami.com.

## *That Fish Was How Big?*
### *Kalkaska*

**H**ere lies a whopper of a fish tale . . . 17 feet long, 12 feet high, more than 320 hours to reel it in. This account isn't fiction. The fact is, those are the statistics of the National Trout Monument.

Constructed in 1966, the work of art commemorates the passage a year earlier of a bill declaring the brook trout as Michigan's official state fish. Those trout bite big in Kalkaska, which has been the home of the National Trout Festival since 1935.

*The trout spouts, twists, and shouts all under colored lights.*

A local grocer, Leo Nelson, had dabbled in some animal sculpture previously and wound up being the one selected to turn out the finished product. Like many artists, he chose to work with his model au naturel: an actual frozen trout.

The fisherman's shrine showcases Nelson's masterpiece emerging from a fountain of colored lights. With mouth wide open, the fidgety fish appears to be leaping for the fly—that is, if the fly's still there. Through the years youngsters have had a good time zipping up the trout and nimbly tackling that fly.

Either way it's a striking tribute to the trout, and it turned out to be the start of a second career for Nelson. Soon afterward, he got his chance to really bring home the bacon, so to speak, when the state of Iowa commissioned him to sculpt a giant 30-foot pig.

Catch the National Trout Monument right in the middle of town on Cedar Street, aka U.S. Highway 131, aka M72, aka M66. For more information, call the Kalkaska Chamber of Commerce at (231) 258–9103.

*E X C L U S I V E L Y   F O R   B I R D ' S - E Y E   V I E W I N G*
*N o r t h p o r t*

**S**hould Alfred Hitchcock ever decide to drop back down from that great moviemaking set in the sky to direct a sequel to *The Birds,* the stage has already been set and the actors are all in their places, though not necessarily ready to go. Thousands of gulls and cormorants have been nesting on a five-acre island just off the shores of Northport since the begin-

ning of time, and it's a safe bet their tail feathers aren't going
to move now.

The island has been a source of trouble for years. Suffering
from an identity crisis, it's universally referred to as Gull
Island, but when first purchased in 1853, it was Trout Island,
then Bell Island, Fish Island, Fisher Island, and Bellow Island,
the official name.

Edward Ustick became deed owner in 1910 and got down to
the arduous task of building his family's dream cottage. The
birds did their darndest at trying to stop the invasion of their
territory, but in a struggle to win this survival-of-the-fittest
challenge, there are stories of Ustick dynamiting the aviary.
Feathers flew, but the birds remained and the home with its
creative plumbing—one pipe laid across the island, entry at one
end, exit at the other—served as a summer retreat until 1942.
Ultimately it was a group of young Northporters, now grown
residents in the area, who entered through an open window
and vandalized the entire property.

Remnants of the house remain—actually only two chimneys, both visible from shore with a good telescope. Everything
else has weathered away, except one tree and, of course, the
birds. They remain victorious over man and island.

In 1995 the Leelanau Conservancy purchased Gull Island
for the purpose of continuing research, which so far hasn't
turned up any news as to why the birds chose this landmass
over others. But no one's going to take it away now. The stench
is repugnant, and even when investigators make it ashore, cormorants have been known to bombard right through at least
one guy's cap, drawing blood. Hard hats are now a necessary
fashion accessory in this modern-day version of *Gilligan's
Island* that's really for the birds.

The Leelanau Conservancy can be reached at P.O. Box 1007,
Leland, MI 49654; (616) 256–9665; or www.leelanau.com/
conservancy/.

# IF THE TREE FITS, SHOE IT

*Y*ou're driving along U.S. Highway 131, M66, just north of Kalkaska, when you notice a confounding sight on the east side of the road. You blink once, then again, attempting to clear your focus, hoping to identify the seemingly foreign objects lacing a wide-spreading tree. What at first appears to be a cluster of brightly colored birds turns out to be none other than hundreds of pairs of shoes embodying the souls of the branches in a nest of high-heeled spikes, sneakers, and boots. Each twosome appears to be gently strung as if they were Christmas ornaments.

Yet it's not a special occasion that causes these heels to kick up the bark: It's an everyday occurrence that commenced with the first sighting in January 2001. Mystery abounds with nary a hint of who or what concocted the idea of the anomalous growth. Whoever is responsible for the botanical bombardment is certainly not a loafer. He's been busy through the years, surreptitiously adding to the mounting number of leather and canvas footwear suspending from boughs. And faithful footwear it is. After one blustery windstorm a fallen branch was seen lying on the ground, still clinging to its inseparable sole mate.

The puzzling shoetree has been the source of controversy, with all eyes on the lookout for the perpetrator. Since the hangings appear to be nothing more than harmless fun, state police say they won't tie themselves into knots trying to horn in on the shoe sower's territory.

*Maybe Elvis is alive. Could these be his blue suede shoes going out on a limb?*

## *ICE DOESN'T FREEZE OUT THE*
## *FAITHFUL*
### *Petoskey*

O n a clear summer day, you may be able to catch a glimpse of the white marble crucifix that's submerged in 25 feet of water off Little Traverse Bay. Or you could wait until midwinter when thousands make the trek to the cross over the ice.

Either way it's a spiritual experience for many and an incredible story to all. It began in 1962 when a father from Bad Axe ordered an 11-foot, one-ton crucifix from Italy for his son's grave. It didn't survive the overseas voyage without damage, so it was refused and eventually offered for $50 in an insurance sale. Purchased and restored by the Superior Marine Divers Club of Wyandotte, the statue was submerged in Grand Traverse Bay on August 12, 1962, as a shrine to all divers, living and deceased. It's believed to be the only underwater crucifix in the Great Lakes.

During the placement, the right arm cracked, broke off, and was taken home by one of the Wyandotte divers for safekeeping until it could be repaired. But before the repairs were made, the diver passed away. So his widow was left holding the right arm of Jesus. She turned the appendage over to Ron Tocco, a fellow club member and avid photographer, who had been part of the original underwater expedition.

In the meantime Dennis Jessick, a young, energetic diver from Harbor Springs, became the new caretaker of the shrine. Determined to find a way to offer landlubbers an opportunity to experience the underwater shrine, he waited until the frozen $H_2O$ was at least a foot deep. Then he painstakingly spent hours with a chain saw, carving out two 6-foot triangles as observation stations. In 1986 the First Annual Ice Viewing of the Underwater Crucifix was held, running from 10:00 A.M. to 10:00 P.M. Jessick says nighttime viewing is the ultimate. A greenish aura casts what some say is a "mystical, enchanting" spell.

While Jessick was thrilled with the overwhelming reception to his frozen pilgrimage, he remained in relentless pursuit of the crucifix's missing right arm.

His efforts paid off when local photographer Bruce Gathman was sharing stories of the ice homage with another photographer, who turned out to be none other than Ron Tocco . . . from Wyandotte. It has to be more than coincidence that for decades Tocco kept the arm, using it as a paperweight.

The answer to numerous prayers came in February 1997, when both Jessick and Tocco's son, Jay, dived down in the bitter-cold waters of Lake Michigan and ceremoniously reattached the right arm of Jesus.

The winter ice viewings take place in February, weather permitting, and throughout the rest of the year divers can view the crucifix in Grand Traverse Bay, just off the pier in Petoskey. For more information, call the Petoskey Visitors Bureau at (800) 845–2828.

## *AQUANAUT SINKS SPIRITS*

*The Superior Marine Divers Club invited the late actor Lloyd Bridges to the dedication of the underwater crucifix in 1962. At the time it appeared to be an appropriate gesture since Bridges was starring in the popular TV series* Sea Hunt.

*The actor's response declining the invitation showed that although he may have been hard at work, it apparently wasn't paying off. The Western Union Telegram was sent from West Hollywood, California* . . . collect.

## MAY THE FORCE BE WITH YOU
### Putney Corners

A desolate country road in northern Michigan has all the trappings for becoming another Blair County prodigy, already endowed with its own cult following. People from all over the state drive to Putney Road for an experience some call mystical, and others simply refer to as baffling.

There's a small section of the road, bordered by cornfields, that seemingly zaps your car backward uphill without any effort on your part at all. Shaking your head in disbelief, like everyone else, you'll try not once but several times over, certain each subsequent attempt will unlock the mystery. It doesn't.

Common sense says the whole thing is an optical illusion. Folklore says the power comes from Blaine Christian Church at the top of the hill, pulling all the sinners back into its fold. Makes sense. No one has left the area without "feeling" the tug.

Although we came pretty close. Giving it that old college try, several times, my husband swore he felt something; I felt nothing. Then a car leaving the only house in sight stopped to give us the bad news. We were on the wrong side of the street.

For guaranteed success, take these directions and a good compass . . . From northbound M31 in the southern portion of Benzie County, go to Joyfield Road. Turn left onto Joyfield and continue to Putney Road. When you see the church, that's Putney Corners . . . Make a left turn, heading south, and drive down to the bottom of the first hill, a few hundred feet, until you can spot the STOP AHEAD sign in your rearview mirror. Drop into neutral, and you'll soon find yourself motoring skyward in reverse. Two important reminders: Be sure you're on the *south* side of Putney, off Joyfield, and that there's not another vehicle behind you. If you do get lost, try reaching the Benzie

County Chamber of Commerce at (231) 882-5801 or (800) 882-5801.

While there's no question the phenomenon is fun, don't you wonder what circumstances provoked someone to discover it in the first place?

## To Float, Empty Your Mind . . . and Other Words by Larry Mawby
### Suttons Bay

A winemaking poet, his claim to fame
The sign out front says L. Mawby's his name
Twelve acres of land with a pen in hand
Become wisdom-laced bubbly, tops in the land*

*Blanc de Blanc*
*She's light, she's lively*
*Blonde and bubbly,*
*She's not French, but her kiss makes your tongue dance.*

Those are the words of Larry Mawby, who's been inking imaginative, free-flowing verse, "most obscene and unprintable," since he was an English major at Michigan State. For the last quarter century, he's also been whipping up liquid spirits in glass bottles and magnums from his vineyard, crediting Senator Ted Kennedy for the opportunity to combine his two favorite forms of palate pleasing.

When the government initiated its policy requiring warning labels on all alcoholic beverages, Larry's outrage would have been good competition for Shaquille O'Neal. It compelled him to tag each product with his personal poetic trademark.

*Not* written by L. Mawby.

Of course the powers-that-be still had to eagle eye every word, and some of those words have raised an eyebrow or two.

*Mille*
*Our fine girl swirl is one in a thousand*
*And a mature-scented-miss*
*mystery with tongue loving curves.*

There were questions on that one, but it passed, as did Turkey Red, Bad Dog, and Tattoo, without one word-smoothing adjustment.

Larry's world is well insulated by his sparkling wines—so much so that while giving a fellow wine maker penny-pinching advice during the purchase of neighboring property, he remained totally clueless. Turns out Tony Ciccione, of Ciccione Vineyards, is "the father of Louise, who happens to have the stage name of Madonna."

For tasting, or to receive a copy of his "infrequent newsletter," reach L. Mawby at 4519 South Elm Valley Road, Suttons Bay, Michigan 49682; (231) 271–3522; or www.lmawby.com.

## *BOTTLE AND FRUIT: EVERLASTINGLY PEARED*
### *Suttons Bay*

First-time visitors to Black Star Farms agricultural estate are incessantly mesmerized by the Pear and its Spirit, a bottle of 80-proof brandy with a large, ripe, perfectly shaped pear lodged permanently inside. How do you get a seemingly unadulterated piece of fruit to fit through the narrow opening? Partner Don Coe quips it's a Clinton pear and he's "taught it to inhale."

*A glass womb bottles up its baby pear, waiting until it gets to drinking age.*

Your eyes cast a glance on acres filled with paradoxical growth, bottles sprouting from branches, convincing you that too much time was spent in the vineyard tasting room. Things aren't always what they first appear to be, and a closer inspection confirms that it's the fruit going through the internal growing pains. Michigan is one of two states in the country (Oregon is the other) where hand-tying bottles to trees is a work of art.

It takes time and some of Mother Nature's blessings to produce the perfect pear, and while the end result is a noble conversation piece, it comes with a price . . . $70 a bottle. It's an exemplary Michigan gift, and even high-ranking state officials have been known to ask for a discount, only to be given the same answer as everyone else . . . no. Why should they get a break when $43 of that price is the tax imposed by the state? This in mind, Coe had an enterprising thought—pass a law making it mandatory for every adult residing in Michigan to purchase one pear in a bottle. As of the 2000 census, Michigan recorded 9,938,444 residents. Assuming two-thirds of them are of legal drinking age, creating a potential influx of an estimated 283.8 million tax dollars, headlines everywhere would read, MICHIGANIANS DRINK THEIR WAY TO STATE'S PROFITABILITY. Might not be a bad idea after all.

The vineyards here sit on the forty-fifth parallel, sharing that distinction with the Burgundy region of France, the two producing grapes that are indistinguishable from one another. Sample for yourself from an extensive selection, including their unique "ice" wines at 10844 East Revold Road. An attractive B&B, equestrian center, and creamery round out the estate. For reservations or information, call (231) 271–4970 or visit www.blackstarfarms.com.

## I SMOOCHED THE MOOSE
### Traverse City

You might be surprised to learn that people drive from hours away to kiss a ninety-year-old moose. But they do. And they've been doing it for years, although no one remembers when the tradition actually began.

Sleder's Family Tavern, believed to be Michigan's oldest continuously operating tavern, opened its doors in 1882. Where once only men sat and drank, today men, women, and children come to enjoy good food and fun.

Part of that fun includes smacking lips with Randolph, a 1,500-pound moose hung on the wall in a traditional kissing mount. Randolph's lovable legend is a mystery, although there have been some theories

*Everyone hears bells ring when they get their first kiss from Randolph.*

that provide fodder for folks. Some hypothesize that puckering up started out as a soccer team initiation. Others say the moose was so big, hunters used to kiss him for good luck on their own pursuit. Bartender Andy Swan says, "It's got to be good luck. Either that or they get the flu."

Whatever the reason, his name is no secret. At a moose naming party one night at the tavern, patrons were asked to applaud for the moniker of their choice. Nothing was clicking with the crowd . . . until one drunk looked at the street sign and yelled out, "Randolph." Everyone loved it. And Randolph he became.

Sleder's Family Tavern is found at 717 Randolph Street, (231) 947-9213. It's open Monday through Thursday, 11:00 A.M. to 11:00 P.M., Friday and Saturday until midnight, Sunday noon to 9:00 P.M.

## MILK HER FOR ALL SHE'S WORTH
### Traverse City

An abandoned set of buildings sit in architectural splendor, vestige of an era many residents today would like to forget. It's the site of the former Traverse City State Hospital, the silent word *mental* fitting in there somewhere, home to hundreds of patients from the late 1800s right through the 1970s.

But one occupant lies down above all others to this very day—Traverse Colantha Walker, the greatest lactating cow ever known to hand, buried on the premises where she was known to really put out . . . 200,114.9 pounds of milk and 7,525.8 pounds of butterfat.

The bountiful bovine contributed more than her fair share to the farming operations, considered therapeutic at the time. Packing 2,000 bushels of tomatoes and 65 barrels of cabbage was thought to render the same effect as Prozac. Other animals

*A giant tombstone marks the grave of Michigan's foremost dairy queen.*

subsidized nutritional needs for poultry and pork, and at one time a huge piggery stood where a junior high school stands today. The local historical society pushed for "Piggery" as the official school name, but that didn't pan out. Instead it became the unimaginatively named West Junior High.

Ms. Walker's monumental tombstone, expressing all her vital statistics, sits at the side of the road, near the barns where she left her mark. A huge banquet was held to commemorate her passing in 1932, where I've heard she was eulogized by guests feasting on royal portions of prime rib.

A local developer has plans for a portion of the main building, but the rest of the complex remains. Located on the west side of Traverse City, west of U.S. Highway 31 (Division Street), north of Meijer Thrifty Acres. Turn west onto 11th Street (watch for the stone pyramid) and continue straight. The noted grave site is on the dirt road (Red Drive) opposite Building 217. For more information, consult www.savebuilding50.org.

Ironwood

Allouez
Laurium · Gay
Houghton · Dollar Bay

41

45

41

141

95

Marquette
Ishpeming
28

Trenary
41

Gladstone
2

41

2

*Whitefish Point*

Paradise
123
Newberry
123
28
Sault Ste. Marie

75

St. Ignace · *Mackinac Island*

BEYOND THE MIGHTY MAC

# BEYOND THE MIGHTY MAC

Admittedly, "Beyond the Big Mac" has a better ring to it, but if there's one thing you don't want to do, it's getting a Yooper ticked, eh, especially if you're a troll. Translation: You don't want to anger a resident of the Upper Peninsula (Yooper) if you're someone who lives in the Lower Peninsula (troll, as in under the bridge).

The Mackinac Bridge, the longest suspension bridge in the Western Hemisphere—approaching 5 miles in length—has been a symbol of unification for Michigan as well as a heck of a good deal for passengers. In 1923, the first year that ferry boats crossed the Straits of Mackinac, 10,351 vehicles were transported to the tune of $2.50 a car. By 1950, 600,000 sets of wheels waited up to twelve hours during deer hunting season and weekends to make that same trip. The delay was permanently eliminated on November 1, 1957, when the "Mighty Mac" opened to traffic. And unlike most fares, this one has gone down over time—today a one-way trip is $1.50. Unless of course it's Labor Day, the one day out of the year when you can walk across for free.

To set the record straight, Mackinac Island is officially a resident of the Upper Peninsula, is always pronounced *Mackinaw*, even though the French spelling throws most people, and sells so much fudge that day-trippers here are affectionately labeled "fudgies."

Besides the sweet smell of confections, the UP is the home of smoked fishy jerky and pasties, a meat pie popularized by the copper miners. You can always pick out the true Yoopers if they pronounce it correctly on the first try. *Pass tee* is the pie, not to be confused with *paste tee* the, um, well, let's not touch that definition. Trust me, there's quite a difference between the two.

Inspired by the environs, you'll find sites like Eckerman's Bear Butt Inn or billboards promoting Moose Joose Koolwater. And coming from a family of Yoopers myself, I can safely say once a Yooper, always a Yooper, curiously summed up on one local license plate as: UP4EVER.

## THE LAST PLACE ON EARTH
### Allouez

In Marketing 101, on the first day of class, the first thing you learn is not to name a store "The Last Place on Earth." It might be a great concept to sell condos in the event of a space invasion, but certainly not what you'd want to call an art, antiques, and collectibles shop.

When Tom and Jan Manniko first purchased their store thirty-three years ago there was, to put it mildly, a little work to do. Even though Tom was a woodworker, his wife, Jan, remembers that when he finished, he said, "I wouldn't do this again if it were the last place on earth." When Jan's friends from Miami asked her about the new venture, she repeated Tom's theme and the name stuck.

With more trees than a woodpecker's fantasy, the Upper Peninsula has a long tradition of woodworking, and the big seller at the store is husband Tom's various types of wooden bowls, plates, and spoons. Each piece is made individually by hand to guarantee a uniqueness that is missing in so much of today's craftsmanship.

Tom has plenty of time to work on his wood carving since the store operates only seasonally, which in this area of the Upper Peninsula means "sometime after the thaw to sometime before the first big snow."

Time seems to take on a different perspective in an area that routinely gets 187.4 inches of snow each year. They don't call it Big Snow Country for nothing.

In fact, back in the winter of 1978–79, Keweenaw County got a record 390.4 inches of snow. That's more than 32 feet.

While Tom is shoveling, snowblowing, and woodworking, Jan has the time to sort out the antiques and collectibles she sells to the summertime folks on their way up to the uppermost tip of Michigan, Copper Harbor.

By the way, for those of you like me who are knickknack-impaired when it comes to collectibles versus antiques, Jan told me that a collectible is technically something between fifty and a hundred years old, while an antique has to be more than a hundred to qualify. The tough part, according to Jan, is knowing the difference between fifty-year-old collectible junk and hundred-year-old antique junk.

You'll find The Last Place on Earth at 59621 U.S. Highway 41. Open 9:30 A.M. to 5:00 P.M. seven days a week. Call (906) 337–1014.

## MORE THAN A FLOOR STORE
### Dollar Bay

They produce a product that is probably used by the most elite group of millionaires in the world. The Horner Flooring Company makes what NBA superstars step onto every night of the season as well as countless practice sessions. Horner floors at high schools and colleges are the "floor of dreams" for thousands of NBA wannabes worldwide.

Back in 1891, when William S. Horner converted an existing pine planing mill to hardwood floor manufacturing, he probably didn't think the company would become the oldest name in hardwood flooring, but by the time he moved the facility from the Lower Peninsula to the Upper in 1914 it was on its way to becoming the world's largest producer of hardwood flooring. Today, at its 60,000-square-foot facility in Dollar Bay, Michigan, Horner makes the Pro-King portable basketball floor that has been used in the NBA all-star games and the NCAA championship play-offs.

If the concept of a portable basketball floor seems strange, you just have to look at the economics of modern arenas. The jump ball at the start of an NBA game tonight might be center stage for a concert by the Backstreet Boys tomorrow night, center ice for a college hockey game on the weekend, and the center ring for the Flying Fannuti Family in a circus the day after that.

Believe it or not, the Pro-King basketball floor used at the Palace of Auburn Hills, home of the Detroit Pistons, Detroit Vipers of the IHL, and more events than even Donald Trump could attend can be installed by the experienced crew there in only six to eight man-hours. The secret is the way the 203 4-by-8-foot panels and 14 4-by-4-foot panels are guided into position and fastened with a hidden sliding lock. It's all part of a patented system that is part of the floor panel itself so it can't be mislaid or damaged. The subflooring allows for changes in humidity for a tight-fitting, level playing surface that means less chance of leg or ankle injuries. What good does it do to have a multimillion-dollar basketball shoe endorsement deal if you have one of your multimillion-dollar feet in a cast?

But don't take my word for it. Ask the Pistons, Nuggets, Jazz, Kings, Celtics, and Trailblazers. The players might not know where the floors are from, but I'll bet they'd be able to identify with anyplace named Dollar Bay.

The Horner Flooring Company is on Avenue H; call (800) 464–7556.

## T*HE* G*AY* B*AR*
### G *a y*

**N**o it isn't. Since the entire population of Gay, Michigan, is only thirty-six people, Bruce and Chris Fountain couldn't afford to cater to any specific group when they bought the Gay Bar after moving to this burg on the shores of Lake Superior.

The town itself is named for Joseph R. Gay, a mining superintendent who christened it in 1936. Back then the saloon was just a place for miners to stop and quench their thirst after a day in the pits.

Although there are gay bars all over the country, there is only one "the Gay Bar." It's a typical Upper Peninsula bar. When you walk in, don't expect to see Richard Simmons impersonators doing a dinner theater version of *Funny Girl*. You're more likely to hear the latest on how the Green Bay Packers are doing. The Upper Peninsula is big-time Packer country, so if you're a Lions fan, prepare to get grief. Of course, if you're a Lions fan, you're used to it.

As for entertainment, Chris says, "We entertain ourselves." Since the bar is horseshoe-shaped, just about any remark triggers a discussion. Despite the town's population, during snowmobile season (which is probably about nine months long) it's not uncommon to see seventy or eighty "sleds" (as the folks around here call them) in the parking lot. In the wintertime the snowmobile trails are used as much as the roads.

The spring thaw brings the annual Gay volleyball tournament, and the Fourth of July Gay Parade draws more than 1,500 people.

Fall saw the First Annual Big Buck Ball contest during which deer hunters who didn't want to lug in antlers were allowed to compete in a much less cumbersome fashion. The

six-and-three-quarter-ounce winning pair was toasted all
around and, we suppose, mourned by the does in the area.

The Gay Bar will soon be up on the Internet, so their big
sellers are going to be available worldwide. They sell assorted
hats, lighters, can coolers, as well as T-shirts that feature car-
toons appropriate for the bar's specialty: a foot-long hot dog.

It's not that Chris and Bruce are greedy. If they were, they
would have decided long ago to start charging for pictures that
every tourist seems to want to take in front of their place at the
GAY BAR sign. Look for the Gay Bar at 101 Lake Street. The
phone number is (906) 296–0951. Open Monday through
Thursday 11:30 A.M. to 11:00 P.M. or "whenever," Friday and
Saturday 11:00 A.M. to 2:00 A.M., Sunday noon to 11:00 P.M.

## *A Tisket, A Casket for Lizards, Snakes, and Squirrels*
### *Gladstone*

**F**inding good entertainment in the Upper Peninsula must be
harder than anyone expected. And just when you thought
you'd heard all the options, along comes someone inviting you
to accompany him on a tour of the Hoegh Pet Casket Factory,
guaranteed to be the only one like it in the universe.

The Hoegh family has been serving the needs of pet lovers
since 1966 with their exclusive line of pink and blue caskets.
As their literature enticingly expresses, this is a golden opportunity to "view the manufacture of pet caskets and tour a
model pet cemetery." Oh, Boy.

Not nearly as dreadful as you might imagine, one of the
company's nine employees takes you through the cookie-cutter
process of transforming a flat sheet of plastic into a vacuum-

*You won't find any dog bones in this cemetery. The rows of
headstones are only "demos" sitting behind the Hoegh Pet Casket
Factory.*

molded casket. Due to the limitations of the molds, no special
orders are accepted, although choices go far beyond a one-size-
fits-all. Dimensions are standardized starting at 10 by 4 inches
to accommodate itty-bitty gerbils or fish, up to the 52-inch
jumbo deluxe, large enough to fit a lion, which on an infrequent basis has been done.

The tours are designed to acquaint people with the concept
of a proper burial for any animal that's been near and dear to
your heart, not just the traditional household cats and dogs,
allowing you, without guilt, to "think outside of the box." The
company acknowledges that their caskets have been the final
resting home for ferrets, lizards, a boa constrictor, squirrels,
skunks, a monkey, and a pet chicken.

Caskets are shipped to 700 locations, some as far away as Puerto Rico and Africa, to the tune of 29,500 a year, not including the 7,500 cremation urns, evidence that this is not a dying business. (I know it's a groaner.)

While it's impossible to keep track of where every casket ends up, a local customer placed a questionable order for a 40-incher for a pet Chihuahua. When confronted regarding the unusual sizing request, she responded, "We wanted extra space so there'll be plenty of room to run around."

Hoegh Pet Casket Factory and Model Cemetery is located at 317 Delta Avenue and is open for tours Monday through Friday 8:00 A.M. to 4:00 P.M. excluding noon to 1:00 P.M. (the staff's lunch break). Call (906) 428–2151 or log onto hoegh.abka.com.

## CARNIVAL—SNOW DIFFERENT THAN RIO
### Houghton

What's a college kid to do in the middle of January watching more than 200 inches of snow fall outside the dormitory window? Celebrate with a bone-chilling cry—"It's Carnival Time."

Being ever so resourceful when it comes to finding a purpose to party, the Blue Key National Honor Fraternity devised the idea of a winter carnival in 1934 at Michigan Technological University, now home to more than 7,000 students.

Like the rhythmic sounds filling the streets of Rio during Carnival, the snowdrifts of Houghton are aflutter with echoes of sizzling-hot irons, buzzing saws, whirling machetes, and a host of other hand tools crafting out chunks of white stuff. Sprinkle in some Jell-O or powdered paint with twenty-eight hours of uninterrupted "engineering homework" and the result is . . . the renowned snow sculptures.

*An all-nighter for students at Michigan Tech turns out chilling*
*artistic beauty.*

The popularity of this time-honored tradition has grown so
that in 2002 school officials instituted a round-the-clock statue
cam over the Internet to satisfy the demand from friends and
alumni worldwide to watch the snow transform before their
eyes, too. An astounding 220,000 people logged on, making
everyone, except the systems director, extremely happy.

The whole carnival scene stretches out for a month, even
though the snow stays quite a bit longer, with human
"dogsled" racing and broomball among the special events. You
haven't lived until you've been exposed to broomball. Students
cut off the sweeper's bristles halfway up, wrap them in duct
tape, then head to the hockey rink in their tennis shoes to
whisk a soccer ball through the goalie's box. Do not try this at
home . . . leave it for the professionals at Michigan Tech.

From time to time the congealment will be joined by a well-known personality. During the selection of the 1939 Winter Carnival Queen, the deciding vote was cast by none other than Mr. White Christmas himself, Bing Crosby.

If you have any questions, you'll get a warm reception from the university's PR staff at (906) 487–2354. Statue cam only operates during Carnival, but the Web site is accessible year-round at www.nu.mtu.edu.

## HIAWATHA TOWERS OVER TOWN
### Ironwood

**O**ne household in Ironwood peers out its front window every day, casting an eye on the world's tallest Indian's backside. Gee, how lucky can you get?

Hiawatha was especially designed for the people of Ironwood in 1964 to attract more attention to the area where the now caved-in iron ore mines once stood, at the end of Burma Street. Mission accomplished. Perched high above the city, everybody enjoys some side of him as he hovers over them. Yet the price for his watchful eye was not cheap. Even back then, his 52-foot-high fiberglass body was constructed to the tune of $10,000.

Traveling through the night so his arrival would be a surprise, the surprise wound up being his disappearance. Hiawatha had been hijacked. Pandemonium broke out, and the national press corps was called in to help pinpoint his whereabouts. Less than twenty-four hours later he was found, safe and sound, with no admission of guilt.

His own special "Erection Ceremony"—the exact words the Hiawatha Committee chose for his official homecoming—went without a hitch as he was anchored into 55 yards of concrete with 5,000 pounds of steel reinforcement while the "Saddleites" circled around on horseback. With the "carnival-like" atmosphere, peddlers were in their glory, hawking special shipments of Hiawatha earthenware replicas from Japan to commemorate the occasion.

Souvenir Hiawatha Banks are currently available through the chamber of commerce for $10.66 including tax. To make a purchase or just to find out more about this friendly Indian with the 26-foot-long peace gesture, call (906) 932–1122 or visit www.ironwoodmi.org.

## DA YOOPER TOURIST TRAP
### Ishpeming

**Y**ooper: (*You-per,* n.) A person from the Upper Peninsula of Michigan.

If there's ever an award for truth in advertising, Da Yooper Tourist Trap wins hands-down. When one of the "hooks" on a billboard to attract customers is FREE BATHROOMS, you don't walk in with high expectations. But surprisingly, those expectations are surpassed.

The first thing you notice when you walk through the corridor into the building is a Yooper museum of sorts. There you can see artifacts of life in the Big Snow Country: what they wore, what they hunted, the type of instruments they played to amuse themselves.

*Amusement* is the key word with the Tourist Trap. It was founded by Jim DeCaire and Lynn Coffey of the band Da Yoopers: a group of Upper Peninsula musicians who have made a real name for themselves singing and fooling around on stages all over Michigan. The band can best be described as a kind of Spike Jones meets Monty Python and moves to the Upper Peninsula. Some of their big hits include "The Second Week of Deer Camp," "Grandpa Got Run Over by a Beer Truck," "Who Goosed the Moose?" and the tender love ballad "Super Dooper

Yooper Love Machine." Their musical style includes everything but good taste. That's not to say it's not entertaining, just not always tasteful.

The marketing job that this store does for the band makes Britney Spears look publicity-shy. In addition to selling their five CDs and eight cassettes, the store sells an assortment of gag products that makes them money off the trolls (people who live in the Lower Peninsula, *under* the Mackinaw Bridge).

After pointing out that the Upper Peninsula has a large Finnish population that "likes to poke fun at ourselves," sales-person Einona Heikkila told me I could purchase a "Yooper cal-culator," which is a small wood cutout of feet with ten toes ($1.95). The "Yooper word processor" is a pencil stub, yours for only $1.50, the "Yooper night-light" is a small tree branch with a candle in it ($3.85), the "Yooper flashlight" is a stick with a match stuck on the end ($1.50), and if you really want to impress your fellow board members at the next big meeting, walk in carrying a "Yooper briefcase": a pair of jockey shorts with handles ($5.95).

You can't miss Da Yooper Tourist Trap: Just look for a truck with a giant shotgun mounted on top. It's found at 490 North Steel Street. Contact (800) 628–9978 or www.dayoopers.com. Summer hours are Monday through Friday 9:00 A.M. to 9:00 P.M., Saturday and Sunday 9:00 A.M. to 8:00 P.M. Hours vary at other times of the year.

## *S CORE  B IG  FOR  THE  G IPPER*
### *L a u r i u m*

**W**hen Ronald Reagan was campaigning for president, the nation united with its rallying cry "Win One for the Gip-per"—a phrase he'd immortalized with his portrayal of George

Gipp in the 1940 movie *Knute Rockne—All American*. Most of those chanting were unaware Gipp, who originally uttered those words, was a born and bred Yooper with unbelievable athletic prowess.

As a University of Notre Dame freshman in 1916, Gipp's first experience in organized football found him drop-kicking a 62-yard field goal. During his tenure in South Bend, he racked up a win–loss record of 27–2 with three ties, personally executing eighty-three touchdowns.

Overall he handled the pigskin far better than he handled books, both overshadowed by his love of wine, women, and song, and in 1919 administrators said adios, voting on his expulsion. A near rebellion broke out on campus, forcing officials to reverse their decision, and Gipp was back tossing the ball, but not for long. A serious throat infection soon found him sidelined.

His conditioned worsened, and it was at his bedside that Coach Rockne broke the headlining news of his selection as Notre Dame's first all-American. To that Gipp responded, "Sometime, Rock, when the team's up against it, when things are wrong, when the breaks are beating the boys, tell them to go in there with all they've got and win one for the Gipper. I don't know where I'll be then, but I'll know about it and I'll be happy."

On December 20, 1920, at age twenty-five George Gipp passed away; his body is buried in Lakeview Cemetery near Calumet.

The Kewanee National Historical Park sponsors walking tours that will escort you to the front door of his birthplace at 432 Hecla Street. A George Gipp monument, fully restored in 1995, sits in the park at the corner of Lake Linden Avenue and Tamarack Street where brick pavers and a flower bed outline the shape of footballs. The folks at the Laurium Chamber are most helpful. Call (906) 337–1600.

# THE WHOLE POOP, NOTHING BUT THE POOP

"*Take this job and shovel it.*" Those are words from Gerry Horn, who was Mackinac Island's chief pooper scooper for thirty-eight years. His job, twelve hours a day, six days a week, was to go around with a wheelbarrow and broom and clean up what the horses left off.

Okay, so the work stinks, but somebody has to do it. With 500 horses on the island, providing the only means of transportation outside of your own two legs, there's a lot of . . . stuff to pick up. The animals don't wear diapers. Putting in seven-hour shifts, the irritation would be too hard on them. Besides, with a constant breeze in the air, passengers would be the ones experiencing a fragrance more like Chanel No. 2.

Sanitation is a peak priority. Each night the streets are completely flushed, and during the day, the shovelers are always on the lookout for business.

But the summer of '02 it wasn't business as usual. A horse-drawn street sweeper was brought in—talk about multiplying your product—and Gerry Horn had to hang up his broom. His eternally optimistic attitude would have made him the ideal candidate for Survivor, quipping, "I may have been voted off the island, but I ain't leaving."

So somebody else will be busy "walking a mile for a pile," and Horn says he'll no longer have to "break my back for a good stack." However, the story has a happy ending for this hardworking gentleman. The king of one-liners has been reassigned, remaining thankful for continuing employment. After all, "it may have been horse poop to you, but it's bread and butter to me."

U

## *LIVERY LICENSES STABLE DRIVERS*
### *Mackinac Island*

**P**arents on Mackinac Island are luckier than most. They don't have to listen to the desperate pleadings for a new car when their children turn sixteen. That's because there are no motorized vehicles of any kind on the island, with the exception of an ambulance, one police car, and two fire trucks. The ban on four wheels officially began as a restriction, permitting them only on tiny French Lane, exclusively during daylight hours so as not to frighten the horses at night. But with the island supported 90 percent by tourism, it was inevitable that charm would prevail. By 1900 tires were out, hooves were in.

And so it is that most youngsters learn to ride a horse before anything else. Rather than the acquisition of a driver's license equating to a national holiday, the monumental stepping-stone is birthday number twelve, with the grand prize a license to operate the preferred winter mode of transportation . . . the snowmobile, a privilege granted here two years earlier than anywhere else in the state.

With a once-a-week dentist and no resident barber, it does become necessary to make the occasional trip to the mainland, so eventually each of the eighty students will need to experience the feel of the open road as seen behind a steering wheel. Thanks to modern technology, driver's education is accomplished via interactive computers. When the big day does come to head over to St. Ignace for some on-the-road experience, it's been said that when pulling up to their first stoplight, rather than putting on the brakes they simply call out "Whoa" to the Buick.

And in case you're wondering if anyone on the island has succumbed to the urge to put the pedal to the metal, the answer is a resounding yes. Longtime resident Mr. Telifson managed to smuggle in two touring cars from the early 1900s. When the governor caught him tooling around under the moonlight in 1948, he claimed the engine was being used only to pump water out of the lake. Oh, thank heaven for automatic sprinklers.

No motors on Mackinac Island—horsepower is the rule not to be broken. The Grand Hotel obliges by transporting its golfers between the lower and upper nine via the country's only horse-drawn golf cart.

## WHAT RIPLEY BELIEVED, GUINNESS DID NOT
### Mackinac Island

There's something about a charming wooden porch that's a guaranteed invitation, whether it's for eats, drinks, or on a rainy day to provide a cover for a spirited game of tennis. At The Grand Hotel, the world's longest columned porch sits majestically overlooking the Straits of Mackinac and, in times of need, has substituted as a home for lobs and volleys. It's certainly big enough, although its exact size has been the source of scrutiny and debate.

In 1936 times were tough, competition for tourism dollars was stiff, and the owner of The Grand, W. Stewart Woodfill—it remains in his family to this day—became a marketing genius almost overnight. With an advertising budget of zero, he invented the claim that the hotel's expansive porch spanned a full 880 feet. For publicity, Robert L. Ripley was contacted, and believe it or not, he fell for the misnomer, spreading the word in his once heralded column. The very next year a line of people 4 miles long waited to sashay across its famed frame.

*In addition to hundreds of rockers, seven tons of potting soil
fills 260 planting boxes containing 2,500 geraniums on
The Grand Hotel's famous porch.*

The record stood for years—forty-six to be exact—until the *Guinness Book of World Records* asked for documentation. Appearing in the fall of 1981 with their own set of surveyors, the measurements revealed the porch was . . . 625 feet. Whoops!

With the latest expansion, the hotel's promenade, accurately computed, fills up 660 feet, although many island tour guides have been overheard continuing to insist it's still 880. Their explanation for the difference? In summer the wood expands, and by the time Guinness arrived, the cool weather had caused a contraction of more than 20 percent.

The popularity of the porch, with its trademark geraniums, has grown so that there's now a charge for non-hotel-guests—$10 a stroll, which can be applied as credit toward the Grand Buffet Luncheon. With 1,000 guests a day paying the extra tariff, it's unlikely The Grand Hotel will ever have to resort to fabricated forms of advertising again.

Street addresses are nonexistent on the island. For reservations, call (800) 334–7263—that's (800) 33–GRAND.

## WAHLSTROM'S RESTAURANT
### *Marquette*

I t looks like any other family restaurant when you're driving along U.S. Highway 41 South just outside of Marquette in the Upper Peninsula. And to most of the regulars, that's exactly what Wahlstrom's is.

Customers around here are used to seeing sweet rolls the size of manhole covers and ordering six kinds of hash-brown potatoes that can include every conceivable topping with the exception of hot fudge. Their standard meat eaters' omelet comes with four eggs, bacon, sausage, ham, cheese, and hash browns inside . . . and a side of pancakes.

When founder Roy Wahlstrom got back to Michigan from the service—he was in the first wave on Utah Beach on D-Day— he got a job as the guard at the prison in Marquette. Knowing that his fellow servicemen were used to getting great prices at the military post exchange stores, he opened a coffee shop and named it The PX.

When Roy noticed that tourists and salesmen were coming to the area and needed a place to stay, he decided to build a motel. While working full time at the prison, he and a carpenter buddy started cutting down trees, clearing the land, and milling the lumber. Before long they had hand-built the first nine motel units and a cafe.

Both prospered, and Roy decided that a restaurant was the next logical step. So in 1960 he built what is now Wahlstrom's.

Roy referred to himself as a busy boy—working up to twenty-three hours a day sometimes. He couldn't have been that busy, though; he still had time for eight kids.

The kids seem to have the same kind of energy level as dear old dad. The eldest, Steve, runs the catering business and is a nonstop promotion machine. The youngest, Tom, is a talented chef.

If you're wondering how talented a chef has to be to make six different kinds of hash-brown potatoes, that's where the catering comes in. Want a sit-down dinner for 1,200? Call Wahlstrom's. Want an entire cow cooked on a spit as a birthday surprise? No problem. Wahlstrom's catering is known for being able to handle everything from a pig roast on the shores of Lake Superior where the supplies have to be brought in by boat, to $100-per-plate dinners served on fine china. Who says you can't be all things to all people?

Look for the restaurant at 5045 U.S. Highway 41 South; (906) 249–1453. Open 6:00 A.M. to 10:00 P.M. seven days a week.

## PAPA BEAR'S HOUSE FITS JUST RIGHT
### Newberry

A typical evening's entertainment in the Upper Peninsula for many years was heading to the garbage dump to watch the bears. With those all closed, the only place you're guaranteed to see bears in northern Michigan anymore is at "Oswald's Dump." Those are Dean Oswald's words, not mine.

He and his wife, Jewel, are the papa and mama of an eighty-acre ranch, the largest ranch in the United States dedicated exclusively to raising bears. Not the most likely career change for someone who spent nineteen and a half years as a Bay City firefighter and a brief stint as a professional boxer, yet knew since the 1950s that this was his heart's true calling.

In 1984 he acquired a license (which you can no longer do in Michigan) and purchased his first bear—appropriately named "Bear"—from a federal breeder in Wisconsin. Along came another one and another one . . . and at last count his family consisted of twenty-five black bears, most trained to come when called, hopefully not too fast since they can run up to 40 mph. Such tender, loving care is administered here that the Michigan Department of Natural Resources sends ailing bears to Oswald for a little R&R (that's "recovery and rehabilitation"). All have done so well they've become permanent residents.

A few questions are probably crossing your mind right about now. The answer to the first one is yes. Dean has been bitten, only once, by Tyson, a 1,000-pounder, who died of a heart attack in July 2000. Question number two gets a no: Jewel doesn't cook all fifty-five gallons of food the clan requires each day. Local restaurants contribute their scraps to help out. The response to number three is sometimes. With the bears in

*Dean Oswald and The Three Bears—at five months old. It's hard to believe they started life the size of a mouse.*

hibernation from late October until the third week in March, the Oswalds are able to have some time away from their beary busy schedule of responsibilities.

Oswald's Bear Ranch is open every day from the Memorial Day weekend through September, 10:00 A.M. to 8:00 P.M. There's a fee per carload, although there's no driving; you walk around all of the ten- to fifteen-acre habitats. From Newberry head north for 4 miles on M123 to Deer Park Road. Turn left and travel another 4 miles. The bear signs will guide you the rest of the way. Call (906) 293–3147 or www.oswaldsbearanch.com.

## *FOLLOW THE BOUNCING BERRY*
### *Paradise*

There's strong evidence that cranberries can either cure or prevent urinary tract infections. If that's true, then the House family, which has been farming them for more than 126 years, must have the healthiest bladders in the world.

Land purchased in 1876 became the Centennial Cranberry Farm, named for our country's hundredth birthday, and has been growing every since, so much that now eighty-five tons of the tart, scarlet gems are harvested each year, most of them shipped out of state and processed into Wal-Mart's private-label juice.

Loren House is the third generation of Houses to till the land of the state's oldest and (until 1993) only cranberry farm, with family members involved in all aspects of the business. His wife, Sharon, oversees the gift shop, situated in the former Whitefish Point Post Office where Sarah House was post-mistress from 1907 to 1916, and in her spare time whips up batches of superdelicious cranberry butter.

Nobody feels "bogged" down, though, since once the vines are in place, they hardly ever need replanting. Recently "native" vines more than a hundred years old were uncovered in a brushy area, still reproducing every three years.

Harvest-time is the busiest, usually occurring mid-October, with the majority of the work done mechanically. All berries are obliged to pass the bounce test—the good ones bounce up, the rotten ones fall to the ground. Kinda reminds me of the pencil test when girls go for their first bra fitting: If the pencil stays, you're ready . . . if it falls to the ground, come back in a few months.

The Centennial Cranberry Farm on 30961 West Wild Cat Road offers self-guided tours every day, noon to 6:00 P.M. from the Memorial Day weekend through October. There's an admission fee per carload; fresh-picked cranberries are $2.00 a pound during harvest only. Call (906) 492–3314.

## VERTICALLY CHALLENGED REDEFINED
### St. Ignace

How many times have you come home from a hard day at work and felt like climbing the walls? When Dan McCarthy's on the job, he's walking up walls every day and watching water flow uphill and balancing chairs on two legs. A magician? Nope. As owner and chief tour guide at the Mystery Spot, he's just doing what comes naturally.

More than 2 million visitors have stopped by since he opened to the public in 1955, but perhaps just as many—like McCarthy's own parents, who decades ago said they "wouldn't stop at that tourist trap"—have driven by still wondering about the puzzling site.

With an inquisitive mind on the quest for the truth, my car came to a halt. Within minutes I found myself walking up a short path, leading to a lopsided shanty where immediately my body felt the mysterious pull. No joke . . . a light-headed queasiness akin to motion sickness set in, which it does for 70 percent of visitors. Clutching the handrails, I was treated to half an hour of mind-boggling, hands-on demonstrations that kept me both scratching my head and laughing hysterically. Who would believe you could be 3 inches taller instantly? Or that a ten-pound pendulum would swing undeniably more uphill? Witnessed with my own eyes, the impossible becomes possible. Questioned whether these are optical illusions,

*Dan McCarthy (left) demonstrates a vertically upright position at his*
*legendary Mystery Spot.*

McCarthy testifies that the Mystery Spot merely accentuates
what nature has already provided.

The story goes that in 1953 surveyors from California were
attempting to level their tripod with a plumb-bob—which was
being incessantly drawn to the east. They soon discovered the
trouble with their equipment existed only in a plot of land some
300 feet in diameter. Which is precisely what you feel when
you're inside the enigmatic zone . . . that tenacious tug to the
east, as if you were magnetized. Once outside the area, their
apparatus worked perfectly, and you'll be back to feeling normal.

After more than twenty years in the seasonal business, the
never-been-married McCarthy says life just doesn't get any better. Named by *Ski Magazine* in 1990 as "ski bum of the year,"

during the winter he heads to Colorado where he hits the slopes for 120 straight days . . . er, make that 116. The last four he goes golfing.

The Mystery Spot is open "rain or shine" from early May through the third weekend in October; hours vary. Call (906) 643–8322. It sits on U.S. Highway 2 West, 5 miles west of the Mackinac Bridge. Admission charge for adults and children five years and older.

## *TAXIDERMY HEAVEN*
### *Sault Ste. Marie*

A bout a third of the way into my Paul Bunyan burger, an ear-piercing siren went off, causing me to nearly jump out of my seat. Blaring lights began to flash, screeching whistles blasted, and a voice came over the PA broadcasting "Welcome from Canada."

It took a few seconds before I realized this was nothing more than a customary salutation from The Antler's Restaurant, one of many I'd hear before my last bite. Anyone can request a bells-and-whistles greeting. Although most are expressing good wishes for birthdays or anniversaries, one lucky guy heard the jolting news, "Congratulations, Darryl, the rabbit died."

Opening its doors first during Prohibition as the "Bucket-of-Blood Saloon and Ice Cream Parlor," the operation was brought to a halt when the IRS learned that profits of $900 were somehow accumulating on the sale of only one quart of ice cream a month. Rumor has it that "The Bucket" earned the distinction of becoming the first lemonade stand in history to refuse to sell to minors.

*Every mammal, fish, and reptile has more than its fill at Antlers.*

After the spot was purchased by two former Detroit policemen, Harold and Walt Kinney, in 1948, a new name went up over the entrance . . . ANTLER'S, for the 300 mounts that eclipse the ceiling and walls. Over the bar you'll find six ducks a-flying, one swan a-swimming, and an anaconda slithered 'round a tree. Elsewhere, expect to encounter trophies of just about every creature that's walked, swum, or flown over the face of the earth, including wild boars, a deer, bison, lions, sharks, a full-sized polar beer, and a furry fish. A new species? The story goes the water in nearby Lake Superior is so cold that even fish find it necessary to grow fur to survive.

The raucousness has brought in hungry revelers from every walk of life, including comedian Bob Goldthwait (who apparently wasn't recognized, since they put him on the wait-

ing list), Motor City madman Ted Nugent, and Farrah Fawcett's
mother (seated immediately). Back in the 1950s, when the
Detroit Red Wings still spent summers training in the Sault,
Antler's became known as the team's second home.

As I walked into the ladies' room, the doorway flocked with
a deer's posterior, I was anxiously awaiting the clever displays
I might find inside. To my disappointment, there were none.
The only mount on the floral-papered walls was a vending
machine dispensing Looney Tunes temporary tattoos.

Antler's Restaurant is open seven days a week, 11:00 A.M. to
9:30 or 10:00 P.M. . . . whenever the crowd decides to go home.
It's located at 804 East Portage Avenue; (906) 632–3571.

## Putting the Word Out
### Sault Ste. Marie

**W**riting anything about Lake Superior State University is
enough to make a writer nervous. After all, this is the
school that every year puts out a list of words they would like
to see banished from the English language.

Get on the wrong side of the powers-that-be and I could
become a wordless writer. Not unlike being a thoroughbred
racehorse put out to stud after a vasectomy.

For twenty-six years Lake Superior State, a school known
for a large male-to-female ratio and a great hockey program,
has put out the "List of Words Banished from the Queen's English for Mis-use, Over-use, or General Uselessness." Every January 1 clichés and catchphrases are banished to the language
junk heap they so richly deserve.

Over the years they've tried to exorcise such oxymoronic
phrases as *free gift* in 1988, and *live audience* in 1983, 1987,

and 1990. Proving that the mere posting on the list doesn't necessarily guarantee linguistic limbo.

The university accepts submissions from the populace at large, and the Public Relations Office gets an "overwhelming amount of submissions." (By the way, if you can be over-whelmed, how many other degrees of "whelme-dom" are there? Just asking, don't put me on the list!)

The 2001 list had a bumper crop courtesy of pundits, poll-sters, and politicians. That year's terms included *fuzzy math*, *chads* of any type, and *negative growth*—which is the diamet-ric opposite of *positive shrinking*.

The world of athletics brings us such gems as *foot speed* and, in my humble opinion, almost any analytical term you hear from a football color commentator with the possible excep-tion of Dennis Miller. Although Dennis is occasionally so con-voluted even he doesn't know what the hell he's talking about, at least he does it with proper English.

*Factoid* made the list, as did *swipe,* as in approving a credit card. *Dotcom* is on the list but they don't care, because before long there aren't going to be enough of them around to complain.

In '02 *friendly fire* left, leaving one to ponder if unfriendly fire would be less painful, along with *reality TV, making money,* (only counterfeiters make it; most honest people earn it), *foreseeable future* (as opposed to the unforeseeable future), and the weatherperson's crutch . . . *Doppler*, causing one Upper Peninsula station to invent its own recipe for "hobbler dobbler peach cobbler."

If you are interested in getting a word or phrase that has you ready to "go postal" (a previous winner), nominations for the future lists along with compelling reasons for banishment should be sent to: Word Banishment Public Relations Office, Lake Superior State University, Sault Ste. Marie, Michigan 49783. Or call (888) 800–LSSU, or visit www.lssu.edu/banished.

# P U S H - A - P O T T Y   P A R A D E
## *Trenary*

The outhouse has been the butt of jokes for years. Recognizing this, the town of Trenary decided to heat up the dead of winter with their own form of bathroom humor. The Trenary Outhouse Classic is the brainchild of lifelong resident Toivo Aho . . . .that's pronounced with a long *a*.

Sharon Fournier, secretary of the Outhouse Classic, says the rules are simple: Build an outhouse with wood and/or cardboard. Put in a toilet seat and a roll of toilet paper. Mount it on skis. Be the first to push it 500 feet and you're a winner.

Of course, creativity doesn't hurt. Since 1993 there have been some outrageous entries. Take, for instance, the White House Outhouse in 1999 with President Clinton sitting on the throne and Monica Lewinsky, walking by his side, attired in her infamous blue dress.

A daffy duo from Munising has been among the biggest crowd-pleasers year after year.

Laurie Walsh and Marcy Heimerman put their two heads together and created the Vat I Can, themselves posing as nuns. Twelve months later they did quite an about-face, reemerging as the Pirates of the Carri pee an, complete with a peg leg that squirted yellow liquid.

Word of the unusual competition has spread nationwide, with contestants traveling from as far away as New York, Virginia, and North Carolina. All for a day guaranteed to provide a lot of laughs and maybe even some extra cash if you're one of the fastest pushers.

*Crowds check out Uncle Sam as he turns red, white, and blue in the face hoping for a heated cush for his tush in his outhouse on Constipation Avenue.*

It's one big party, with the town of 550 swelling to more than 3,500 that last Saturday in February. Crowds line Main Street for the Privy Parade. When it's all done, mobs enjoy a game of volleyball in one of the huge snowbanks. Others may head over to the Silver Dollar or Trenary Tavern for a couple of pops.

If you're thinking of participating, you might want to bring along your golf shoes. It's not easy pushing an outhouse on ice, and those spikes may just come in handy to give you some much-needed traction.

For an application or to learn more about the Hoity-Toity event, call (906) 446–3504 or write Outhouse Classic, P.O. Box 271, Trenary, Michigan 49891.

## *Trenary Toast;*
## *Shelf Life — Eternity*
### *Trenary*

**F**orget about twice-baked potatoes. You haven't lived until you've tasted the popular twice-baked bread known as Trenary Toast. It's the creation of the Trenary Home Bakery, an establishment housed in its original building from 1930, although there have been several additions since to accommodate the growing demand for the UP staple.

The Siiranen family was the first owner; they sold it to Hans and Esther Hallinen in 1950, who've kept it in their family for three generations. Its current owner, grandson Joseph Hallinen, gives the real credit for twice-baked bread to the Vikings, who developed the technique centuries ago.

However, the recipe has remained the same . . . Take sweet white bread. Bake it. Add cinnamon and sugar. Bake it again.

*Staring at a plate of Trenary Toast can cause an adrenaline rush
for multitudes of hungry fans.*

Keep it in an airtight container and you can enjoy it forever. Or almost. Even though the official guarantee is for six
months, it's been known to last for years. On Day 1,274 it
tastes exactly as it did on Day 1.

On your first bite, you'll say it's hard. It's supposed to be.
Think of it as a Finnish biscotti, and use it to dunk in your
coffee.

People all over the country enjoy the toasty treat, with
3,000 bags going out weekly. A ten-ounce bag containing ten
to fourteen pieces will set you back $2.75.

The Trenary Home Bakery ships to all fifty states, but does supply some retail outlets in lower Michigan. And no, they don't use any preservatives; the trick is all in the baking. You can visit them at E2918 Highway M67. Dial (906) 446–3330 or (800) 862–7801, or log onto www.trenarytoast.com. Open Monday through Friday 7:00 A.M. to 3:00 P.M.

## DAVEY JONES LOCKER OF THE GREAT LAKES
### Whitefish Point

**O**pening the doors, the first poignant strains of Gordon Lightfoot's version of "The Edmund Fitzgerald" can be heard breaking through. Your eyes hone in a large brass bell, emblazoned with the words EDMUND FITZGERALD, retrieved almost twenty years to the date after the mighty freighter sank in the waters of Lake Superior just 17 miles from where you now stand.

It is to this and the other 6,000 ships lost on the Great Lakes that the Shipwreck Museum at Whitefish Point pays tribute. Thirteen different shipwrecks are recapped—no explanation for the odd number—ranging from the *Invincible* in 1816 to the *Fitzgerald's* 1975 demise. Selected artifacts from each are displayed: hats, glasses, binoculars, even a gold wedding ring, telling their own tales of the 80-mile area just outside that's come to be known as "Shipwreck Coast" due, in part, to the perpetually high winds and treacherous weather conditions.

On a somewhat brighter note, the museum is filled with magnificent shadows cast off the 344 crystal prisms of the bigger-than-life Fresnel lens. Each is so precisely arranged that

*A 17-foot-tall Fresnel lens with a range of 28 miles stands guard over the actual bell retrieved from the* Edmund Fitzgerald.

even a modest source of light is refracted into an intense beam visible for more than 28 miles.

A somewhat daunting and thought-provoking afternoon can be spent inside, pondering the two questions that have never been answered: Why did the lighthouse fail to shine on November 10, 1975, the night the *Fitzgerald* and her twenty-

nine-member crew went down? And why did it go out again on
July 4, 1995, the night the divers returned with her bell?

For a true feel of the mystery surrounding Whitefish Point,
you can spend a night in the crew members' quarters, built in
1923. Fully renovated, rooms are $150 a night after you pay
the $25 membership to join the Whitefish Point Shipwreck His-
torical Society.

Follow M123 to its northernmost end; a dirt road will lead
you the rest of the way.

The museum, including a fascinating video and tour of the
lighthouse, is open daily from 10:00 A.M. to 6:00 P.M., May 15
through October 15. Admission is charged. For more info or
reservations, call toll-free (877) SHIPWRECK or visit their Web
site, www.shipwreckmuseum.com.

## THE MIDDLE FINGERS

# THE MIDDLE FINGERS

**P**lease note that the chapter is "Middle fingers," with an *s,* plural, more than one. This is an expansive area of Michigan, protruding to the northernmost tip of the Lower Peninsula incorporating index, ring, and, yes, middle finger. This is the region most commonly thought of when you hear people say they're going "up north," allowing room for some crossover into the pinkie.

Prime deer hunting territory, each November, I–75 (aka speed trap heaven) jams up with more camouflage outfits than the U.S. Army, on their way to combat duty in the woods. Year-round, waterways, too, are filled with those setting their sights on nabbing the big one that got away.

Yes, we do love our animals, if only to admire them from afar. The state's biggest elk population resides in Otsego and Montmorency Counties, and while there are no pigeons in Pigeon River, you're more likely to catch a glimpse of a sturgeon in Black Lake than you are on Sturgeon River.

It's a safe bet that this is the only place in the world where you can walk inside a dinosaur, pork out on the golf course, and come face to face with a man-killing clam. You have to be in tip-top physical condition merely to be an onlooker at one of the annual sporting events here.

Gene Taylor made his second home in this region—fondly labeled "the Sunrise Side"— where he savored the splendor of radiant morning skies as only a true morning person could do.

Contrary to Charlie Brown's saying "Morning people are hard to love," after experiencing the delightful idiosyncrasies of the people, places, and things of Michigan's northeast, before long, it will be obvious why each new dawn is blithely greeted with a three (middle) finger salute.

### RUDY
### Alpena

The thing that makes any small-town bar interesting is the same thing that makes a small town interesting: the people. Bartenders, be they male or female, are a cross between a rent-a-friend, traffic cop, marriage counselor, and father confessor. Frank Sinatra got rich singing lines like "So set 'em up Joe, I got a little story you ought to know."

The sign on the outside might say 10TH AVENUE INN or THE PUMP, but people in Alpena, Michigan, know it as Rudy's. Who would have thought that the best pork ribs in the universe would be found at a bar in Alpena? But don't take my word for it. It's there in black and white on the sign in front. As Rudy says, "As soon as somebody from another planet comes in with pork ribs that taste better than ours, I'll change the sign."

Rudy Beegan is the first to admit his being a bar owner in Alpena is a mistake. "I'm in the sixth year of a three-year plan for this place. I bought it from one brother and I'm selling it to another brother."

That's the plan. But things seldom go according to plan for Rudy. He got his bachelor's degree at Eastern Michigan University and his master of fine arts degree at the School of the Art Institute of Chicago. Although opening a beer or mixing up a Jack Daniel's and soda won't get you in a gallery, Rudy feels that "anything you do well is art."

The world according to Rudy is a fascinating place, and the regulars there seem to affirm his Yoda-like status. One woman came in and ordered a Budweiser and handed him a ring that she said was a family heirloom. Not for payment, for appraisal. No problem. Rudy reached in back of the cash register, pulled out a jeweler's loupe, and proceeded to give her a complete evaluation.

Rudy says he's spent the first fifty years of his life "filling his toolbox with skills." The second fifty he'll spend "assembling it all," and the third fifty he'll "sit back and relax and enjoy it all."

Rudy has been telling people he's leaving Alpena ever since he got there but don't blame me if, by the time you read this, he's back in Morocco. He once spent four years in Tangiers working as a plumber. Then again, if you're at a pub in Tangiers, they might tell you that Rudy just left yesterday for the Pump in Alpena.

The 10th Avenue Bar is on U.S. Highway 23 at 900 West Chisholm. Open Tuesday through Saturday 2:00 P.M. to 2:00 A.M. Call (989) 356–9357 for more information.

## HAM IT UP AND OUT
### *Atlanta*

**M**ichiganians are the biggest swingers in the country. Now don't get teed off by that statement until you hear all the facts. According to statistics from the National Golf Foundation, the mitten state has the nation's highest percentage of residents over the age of twelve who play the frustrating "chase-the-little-white-ball" game. Yep, 20 percent of all Michiganians hit the links, or the sand traps, or other things they're not aiming for. And if you need to know how you fare against a typical golfer, that's been defined as a just-over-forty-year-old male who plays twenty-two rounds per year, shooting an average of 97.

Stepping out of character is the tenth hole of Elk Ridge Golf Club, a 450-acre public course designed by Michigan architect Jerry Matthews. From the tip of the tees to the tip of the green there's an elevation change of 100 feet, providing panoramic views of the north and an increased opportunity for nosebleeds. What uniquely marks this hole is the front right bunker, a real bear to get out of, as the sand appears ready to snort from its shapely snout. Your vision's fine: Staring you in the face is the shapely physique of a pig. Not a wild boar, but a Porky-style pig.

Always good for a few laughs, foursomes have been known to bet against the squiggly tail—whoever hits into it buys everyone a round of . . . ham sandwiches.

The pig's existence is courtesy of Lou Schmidt, who as owner of both the course and the Honey Baked Ham Company has proven he's not only a fanatical golfer but also a bona fide publicity ham.

For nongolfers, pig viewings are available from the tepee-style clubhouse at Elk Ridge Golf Club, 9400 Rouse Road, 6 miles north of Atlanta off M33. Call (989) 785–2275 or (800) 626–4355.

### KINGFISH OF KITSCH
#### Cheboygan

Leslie Earl: She sells seashells, not by the sea, but right off I–75, at Exit 326. The unlikely location of this oceanic emporium known as Sea Shell City has been wooing devotees since 1957. As only the second proprietor in its nearly half-century history, Earl doesn't seem fazed that this tropical merchandising paradise sits in the heart of northern Michigan. After all, "Not everyone can go to Florida, so they come here instead."

Almost as well known as the business itself are the eleven billboards lining the preceding 40-mile stretch of freeway, with adrenaline-rushing captions STOP AND SEE CAPTAIN HOOK, ONE MILLION SHELLS, and the clincher . . . FREE ADMISSION TO VIEW THE GIANT MAN-KILLING CLAM.

Once inside the 8,000-square-foot, meticulously maintained galley of gifts, the assortment is wider than the Atlantic and

*Leslie Earl could have easily shelled out a clambake for the entire population of Michigan with this 505-pound beauty.*

Pacific combined. Shoppers weave through aisles filled with unrelated trinkets: nautical novelties, T-shirts espousing the benefits of Michigan roadkill, sponges, Gummi Sharks, and rows and rows of bins hemorrhaging every type of shell ever known to sand.

A few feet beyond the saltwater aquarium is the proclaimed pièce de résistance . . . the mammoth clam. Yes, it's a real clam, though it hasn't been alive in at least forty-seven years. Purchased in the Philippines, it weighs in at 505 pounds and— though I hate to disillusion you— couldn't possibly have devoured anyone. Clams are vegetarians. But you'll never see one bigger. That is, unless you're the culprit who a few years ago took the 700-pounder out of the parking lot.

Sea Shell City, at Exit 326 off I–75, will occupy more than a few minutes, giving the kids a chance to stretch their legs on the pirate ship outside. It's open 9:00 A.M. to 5:00 P.M. seven days a week from April 1 through the third weekend in October; from mid-June through Labor Day it stays open until 8:00 P.M. Call (877) 435–5248 or hook on at www.seashellcitymi.com.

## *WANTED: STURGEON-SITTERS, NO EXPERIENCE NECESSARY*

*In these parts they take their sturgeon seriously, and for good reason. With its prehistoric origins, some say looking into the eyes of the largest freshwater fish anywhere is like looking into the eyes of a dinosaur. It's a threatened species, and Cheboygan's determined to do whatever it takes to preserve the 8-foot, 200-pound centurions that make their home in Black Lake.*

*A round-the-clock sturgeon protection program during spawning season has 350 volunteers who spend 3,800 hours wrapped in blankets at night with video cameras in hand, guarding the fish from those who want to poach the eggs for caviar. Maybe not the most exciting line of work, but at least the fish don't talk back or give you trouble at bedtime.*

*Then, in what could be considered a paradoxical move, each February since 1948 about 1,000 people wait in line for one of the twenty-five daily sturgeon tags that come available. A lottery decides the chosen few who will venture out on the ice for a chance to spear one of the five fish they've been licensed to kill.*

*So how long does it take to capture five struggling sturgeons? In 2002 it took a full twelve days. But the record was set the year before, in 2001. With barely enough time to lace up your boots, the quintet was rounded up in just thirty-five minutes.*

*For more information on any of the sturgeon programs, contact the Sturgeon General, Brenda Archambo, through the Web site www.sturgeonfortomorrow.org.*

## Legs Still Standing Thanks to Polish Indian Chief
### Cross Village

**N**a zdrowie! Those were the words spoken in 1921 by a thirty-four-year-old Polish immigrant as he raised his glass in a toast to his new neighbors, the Ottawa Indians of Cross Village. The bonds of brotherhood grew strong, and the local tribe's chief, having no male heirs, took in Stanley Smolak as one of his own, bestowing upon him the Indian name of Chief White Cloud.

In gratitude for the wonder and beauty of his adopted land, Chief Smolak used his dexterity to build the two-story Legs Inn, a feat accomplished with only his two hands and all the stumps, limbs, roots, and stones that nature could provide. With one exception . . . the legs. They're actually legs of stoves, which he inverted to form the decorative railing on the roof. Hence the name *Legs Inn*, although it might be better suited to *Legs Up*.

The extraordinary complex is operated today as a restaurant by Stanley's nephew, George Smolak, and his wife, Kathy, serving up helpings of golabki, pierogi, lasanki, and bigos (a Polish hunter's stew), which you can wash down with one of a hundred different beers. Of course, if you're worried about your Polish pronunciation you can always order the cheese nachos.

It may seem a little odd at first to see someone from Italy or Taiwan in a traditional Polish costume walk up and ask you if you'd like some nalesnik, but Legs proudly participates in an International Cultural Exchange Program, exposing all nations to a taste of the Polish side of Michigan.

*Struggle is the unusual name given to one of the unique woodcarvings lining the interior of Legs Inn.*

This is the one place where you actually hope there is a line to get in, so you can linger in the manicured gardens where the view over Lake Michigan is as close to heaven as you're likely to get on earth. Time it right and you'll catch a captivating sunset that's more than worth the wait. Or better yet, try to get one of the dining tables outside and then raise your glass in a "Hail to Chief Smolak." *Smacznego!*

Getting to Legs Inn from Harbor Springs is a memorable drive through M119's "Tunnel of Trees." It's located in the heart of Cross Village at 6425 Lake Shore Drive; there are no reservations. Open mid-May through the third week in October for lunch and dinner. Phone (231) 526–2281 or visit www.legsinn.com.

## SOMETHING FISHY AT LIXEY'S
### East Tawas

There is a proverb that says, "Give a man a fish, and he'll eat for a day; teach a man to fish, and he'll open a fish market." At least that's the way the Lixey family heard it.

Don Lixey will tell you that the sign outside Lixey's Fish Market off U.S. Highway 23 isn't exactly accurate: The family hasn't been operating a fish market at the current location since before the Civil War. But Don's grandfather Joseph Lixey *was* selling fish back in 1860. Don's father Henry took over the business of, according to Don, "just catching and selling fish." At that time the fish were salted instead of frozen, but as Don says, "Fish are fish."

With the exception of a 200-pound sturgeon, the product then was much as it is today: lake trout, herring, whitefish, and perch.

Although the market is open to retail buyers, the mainstay of the business is the area restaurants and stores. Up until the 1950s when the railroad stopped shipping, Lixey's sent fish as far away as New York. That was about the time that there was some worry about the Great Lakes being fished out. But thanks to conservation and some limits on fishing, there seems to have been a comeback.

Any of the locals who have been there lately will tell you the market is a little different now, even though the choice of fish is still "whatever Mother Nature gives us," according to Bud, one of the local fishermen. These days you can at least see the fish displayed before you in a sparkling white cabinet. They've even added a shelf full of cocktail and tartar sauce. But the building still looks pretty much like a big garage.

That makes sense, because you have to drive down a long winding dirt driveway off U.S. Highway 23 and follow the signs. Then get rid of the "It-can't-be-back-here" feeling you get driving past residential homes.

Business is still good at Lixey's even though the old-timers would have a tough time believing the perch now appear on menus at area restaurants with the "if-you-have-to-ask-you-can't-afford-it" notation "Market Price."

And it doesn't hurt that you can't turn on the TV or pick up a magazine without being told that eating fish is going to make you healthier, smarter, sexier, and live longer.

Since Don Lixey was born in 1921, he'd probably be the first to tell you those stories must be accurate.

Lixey's Fish Market is on U.S. Highway 23 north of East Tawas—just follow the signs. Open 9:00 A.M. to 5:00 P.M. seven days a week. Call (989) 362–5791.

## STAN THE MAN
### East Tawas

He's there when they open. He's there when they close. He doesn't cause any problems and nobody ever has to drive him home. At Chum's Bar in East Tawas, you might call Stan the perfect regular. Stan loved the gang at Chum's and wasn't about to let a little thing like dying get in the way of hanging out there. When Stan finally got the ultimate last call December 5, 1998, it seemed only fitting that part of his ashes ended up in an empty bottle of his beloved Imperial whiskey in a place of honor behind the bar.

Anna Busch owns Chum's, a local watering hole that's been in the family for fifty-two years. These days the tourists are more likely to order a margarita or ask to see the wine list than the Imperial whiskey on the rocks that Stan Humphrey favored. When Stan dropped by Chum's after a day of selling used cars at his lot on U.S. Highway 23, there weren't the touches that you see now: the espresso machine that's just a short distance from his perch, the electronic darts game, the big-screen TV, or the bottles of Chambord or Godiva chocolate liqueur. Back when he first came in, Stan was lucky to get popcorn as opposed to the "Acorn squash–covered Chicken" or "Kathy's Krab Sandwich" that are on the menu now.

In 1920 half of what is now Chum's was Aunt Fran's Lunch Counter. She sold it in 1930 to her brother Chumie Kleanow. In 1933 when Prohibition ended, the bar got one of the earliest liquor licenses issued by the state (it has zeros in front of the number). Chumie rented out the bar to various operators until 1946, when it was Rita's Place. She got into a disagreement with the liquor commission, who forced her to sell it. It became Chum's that year. Even now there's a 1948 phone book on the wall at Chum's, and because everybody had the same exchange in town, some of the phone numbers are only one digit. Chumie ran the bar until his death in 1956, when it was taken over by his son Billy Kleanow, Anna's former husband.

Stan Humphrey saw it all. Stan hailed from Hale, Michigan, a short distance across M55 and he started stopping by Chum's in 1934 at the age of eighteen (liquor laws weren't quite as strict in those days). His work schedule permitted him to stop by the bar when things were slow at the used-car lot, and the word was that Stan probably sold as many cars out of "Chum's branch office" as he did at the dealership.

After he retired, Stan stopped by Chum's every morning to make sure everything was right with the world, had a couple of drinks, and then headed out until he returned for cocktail hour about 4:30. He became so much a part of the Chum's family that Anna became his unofficial guardian, and when he didn't show up or Stan's four adult children couldn't get in touch with him, Anna was the contact. When she suggested that she wanted some of his ashes as a tribute after her buddy retired to that long bar in the sky, Stan said, "What the hell for?" She said it just made sense and the place wouldn't be the same without him. Stan said, "Ask the kids," and when they approved, a shrine was born.

Although Anna has put Chum's up for sale, things probably won't change much. The eventual new owners will have to agree that Stan is part of the deal. He's become a celebrity in his own right with people stopping by to say hello and have a shot of Imperial in his honor. Every year in mid-July, Stan's family and friends gather in East Tawas for a golf outing and party in Stan's honor. But nobody at Chum's ever has to worry about things getting out of control. After all, kids know to behave when their dad is in the room.

Chum's Bar is located at 105 West Westover; (517) 362–3681. Open Monday through Thursday noon to 9:00 P.M., Friday and Saturday noon to 11:00 P.M., Sunday noon to 8:00 P.M.

*Stan Humphrey never leaves the bar, even at closing time. His remains sit inside this bottle of Imperial whiskey on a shelf at Chum's.*

# TAWASES' TALES TELLER

**W**hen you walk into The Booknook bookstore on
Newman Street in East Tawas, the sign over the
second counter in the middle says it all: MEET THE AUTHOR
BEHIND YOU. Naturally you look around for the little
table bookstores always set up for some poor writer to
sit at, pen in hand, waiting for someone to buy a book
so it's creator can scrawl some kind of inscription. It's
the literary counterpart of trick-or-treating.

But in this store, there's no table to be found, nor is
there a publisher's flack to cater to their writer's whim
for a glass of water or a better chair.

If author Neil Thornton wants a glass of water, he
has his publisher get it for him, or the store owner, or
the guy working the register. In other words, he gets it
himself.

Tawas City and East Tawas are kind of the twin
cities of the sunrise side of Michigan. If you want to
know why there are two Tawases, writer Neil Thornton
is the man to ask.

Thornton was literally born into the writing business. His dad owned the weekly Tawas Herald newspaper
in Tawas City, and his birth over the offices in 1928
might have given new meaning to the term free home
delivery.

Even so, Neil became a writer by accident. He went
into the army during the Korean conflict as a rifleman,
but thanks to "military intelligence" it was assumed
that anybody who grew up in a newspaper office was
automatically a reporter. Neil quickly realized that the
pen was not only mightier than the sword but also a
heck of a lot lighter than a rifle. So he spent a nine-
month tour of on-the-job training writing for the Army

Times. *After returning from the Army to Michigan, he and his brother bought his father's interest in the newspaper in 1955, which they ran until they merged with the* Iosco County News *in the early 1980s.*

*Neil bristles at the theory that "today's newspaper is tomorrow's fish wrapper." With a newspaperman's pride he says, "Today's newspaper is tomorrow's history."*

*Local history had always been Neil's passion, so in 1981 he turned a feature story he wrote on the lumber industry into a book called* Log Marks. *He thought that title wouldn't exactly jump off the page to a publisher, so he published it himself. The following year a book on railroading called* High Iron along the Huron Shore *continued his one-man publishing empire.*

*Today, thanks to computers, self-publishing is just a matter of the right hardware, unless you're a newspaperman at heart. That's why Neil does all his "the old way." He writes his manuscripts on an old standard Underwood typewriter, sets all his own type in linotype, pulls proofs, runs them on a fifty-year-old office duplicator, and prints his covers on a hundred-year-old press. When you buy one of Neil Thornton's books, you're not only reading history, you're holding it in your hands.*

*Even though his fifteen books are ordered from all over the country, and his railroad books have been sought by readers as far away as Germany, don't look for Neil Thornton's Web site on the Internet. He hasn't set anything up yet. He's too busy writing, printing, and working behind the counter of The Booknook, where you'll still find him every Saturday, selling and telling the tale of two Tawases. The store is found at 114 Newman Street; call (517) 362-4691. Open Monday through Saturday 9:30 A.M. to 5:30 P.M., Sunday 11:00 A.M. to 3:00 P.M.*

## ONE POTATO, TWO POTATO, BURGERS
## FOR ALL
### Elmira

It's a convenient way to get three and a half weeks' worth of your body's nutritional requirements for carbohydrates and cholesterol. Two or three bites max of the state's only potato burger should do the trick.

Now, a potato burger wouldn't be my first choice if it were buried in the middle of the menu. However, the Elmira Inn is the *home* of the original potato burger so it seemed foolish not to give it a try. I wasn't disappointed, but give my gastrointestinal tract a few hours to respond.

Kelly (real name Caleen) Niedling used her culinary talents to whip up the concoction of shredded potatoes and ground beef, prefried so the whole thing doesn't fall apart, dipped in a beer batter, and finally given a full dunk into the deep-fryer before it's slapped on a bun. Reminds you of a twice-fried shepherd's pie that's been double-dipped in the fryer.

The Elmira Inn celebrated its centennial a few years back, though the present structure is only thirty-five years old. The original bar stood right across the street until it burned down, forcing relocation.

Of everything inside—pool table, dartboard, et cetera—the potato burgers, at twenty years old, may be the youngest. Thanks to bikers, both peddlers and motored, who crave their carbs, after a recent marathon the cash register rang up a belly-busting 200 PB's in one day, leaving one to wonder if folks were totally "mashed" when they left.

A potato burger goes for $4.50. Tack on another quarter for cheese. Unless you're famished, take Kelly's advice—share it with a friend. Elmira Inn is on M32, 2 miles east of U.S. High-

*Kelly Niedling delivers one of her signature potato burgers amid a backdrop of onion rings. (Yes, there is just one—it's been cut in half.)*

way 131 on the south side of the road. The official address is 501 Underwood, though that's the side street and there isn't a side door. Phone (231) 546–3248. The hours are 11:00 A.M. to 2:00 A.M., but if they're not busy, they'll close at midnight.

# BULLWINKLE WOULD BE PROUD

*H*orns aplenty: moose, caribou, elk, deer. They're all in Bob Mowery's workshop in Frederic, waiting for his steady, skillful hands to turn them into something more than the natural works of art they already are.

Bob's hours of laborious work with a Dremel air turbine drill, whirling twice as fast as that of a dentist, give a run-of-the-mill antler an architectural overhaul into a tableau of wilderness wonders. He doesn't add anything; he merely subtracts layers of the shredded-wheat-like interior to form eagles, bears, pine trees, or anything else that one of his clients may envision.

Due to the intensity of the work and the health risks involved—gas-mask-type covering is necessary to prevent calcium from settling in his lungs—a year's worth of work turns out a limited thirty to thirty-five pieces. But once one is completed, the artistry confirms it's worth the wait.

Mowery had quite a wait himself before digging into bones full time. For eleven years he measured big-game antlers for Commemorative Bucks of Michigan, with several discoveries scoring 170 or more in the Boone and Crockett system. He had no formal art training, but "drawing just a little bit" one day, he decided to try his hand at doing more with the animal racks he had come to know so well. The try turned out to be a big success.

Apparently right-brain-dominant forever, Bob's musical talents had earlier found him composing music for Caprice records. A Kenny Rogers album features one of his hits, "I'll Always Love You." Maybe that's what Bullwinkle is singing to him right now.

You can reach Michigan's only antler artist serving the public at (989) 348–6290; write to 5779 North Weaver Road, Frederic, Michigan 49733. At Bob's place it's either BYOA or he'll supply one for you.

*The buck stops here . . . for a makeover in the crafty hands of Bob Mowery.*

## FRED BEAR'S ALL TO LOCAL COLLECTOR
### Frederic

**P**ete Kocefas switches hats faster than a juggler in a three-ring circus. One minute he's answering his phone "Sled-head's Snowmobiles"; the next it's "First Impressions"—his sign company—or he could be greeting the caller with "Wayside Inn Cottage," a rental property. Summing it up best are the words inscribed on one of the many posters he has of his hero, FRED BEAR—RESTLESS SPIRIT.

The Grayling area has been having a love fest with Fred Bear and his archery equipment ever since his manufacturing plant went up in 1939, when it employed some 400 people. Almost everyone in town was involved with the company in one way or another, and there were dark clouds overhead that dismal day in 1978 when the operations were transferred to Florida. The Fred Bear Museum continued to operate for two years beyond that before tearfully shutting its doors locally, too. With a worldwide reputation, people to this day still stop and ask how to find it.

That's why Kocefas stepped in, to continue paying tribute to the man who used to walk the downtown streets daily and stop and talk to anyone he passed. It started out as a collection of a few bows, but word spread quickly; and it wasn't long before anyone in Grayling who found something of Bear's in a closet would instantly cry out, "Call Pete." A sampling of newly acquired pieces occupies a corner of Kocefas's snowmobile shop. One of the first Fred Bear museum T-shirts sits folded in its original plastic wrapper with a price tag of $5.50. That's what it cost years ago—none of the collection is for sale today, nor will it ever be, as the hobby is strictly an expression of respect and admiration.

While several bows hang out in easy eyesight, the larger "shrine" is set up in the back workroom. Here you'll find another 150 arrow propellers artistically surrounding numerous Fred Bear posters, a feather barrel (the contents remain untouched), and hundreds of trinkets ranging from Fred's own hatpin collection to his personal hunting knife crafted in Africa, covered in nothing less than lion fur.

Always on the lookout for anything that Bear ever touched, one day Kocefas and his nine-year-old daughter were doing their own excavation of the site of the bygone museum when she frustratingly asking, "Dad, you're not thinking of getting that toilet seat?" Up popped a scheming twinkle in his eye, leaving one to only imagine what happened next.

Kocefas is always willing to share his enthusiasm with interested parties. Most winter days you can catch him at Sledhead's, 6636 South Old 27. Otherwise his sign states, SUMMER HOURS BY APPOINTMENT OR WHEN MY TRUCK IS HERE. You'll know it's his if the back reads BEAR ARCHERY COLLECTOR. Call him at (989) 344–7669—that's (989) 344–DIGSNOW.

# THIS SPORT'S A HOOT FOR NIGHT OWLS
## Grayling

On Saturday, September 6, 1947, the Au Sable River gave birth to a set of twins: the world's longest marathon canoe race and the world's toughest spectator sport. No one was quite ready for the second seed to become as prominent as it has, but for more than fifty-five years now, thousands of people have been following two-person teams paddling 120 miles nonstop from Grayling to Oscoda. A perfect outlet for insomniacs, the competition begins at 9:00 P.M. and runs for fourteen to nineteen straight hours.

*Thousands of fans line the banks of the Au Sable to catch a fleeting glimpse of the fleet of paddlers.*

And what a beginning it is. With a hundred participants all lined up, 10 feet apart, the cannon explodes, signaling a run-for-your-life mad dash toward the narrow (just 20 feet) opening of the river, while crowds scream wildly on shore.

All night long the excited devotees line the banks of the river to cheer for the athletes, who come from twenty-two different states and at least one foreign country. It's hard to tell who's in better shape since top-notch strength and stamina are requirements for involvement on either side of this marathon. Instead of late-night bar-hopping, it's bridge-hopping that's going on with an equal amount of rowdiness.

The course itself isn't easy even in daylight, with many obstacles to circumvent including six dams, each forcing paddlers out of their boats to sprint over uneven, slippery terrain. So the teams' bank runners come equipped with everything from Band-Aids to flashlights to duct tape (which has been used on several occasions to mend a boo-booed boat).

No matter what the outcome, it's always wildly fun and rewarding recreation; those who participate once say it's hard not to experience it again. Just ask Al Wilding Sr. from Mio, who in 2002, at age seventy-seven, paddled in his thirty-first Au Sable Marathon.

The race is now held the last weekend in July. Information is available by calling (989) 348–4425 or visiting their Web site at www.ausablecanoemarathon.org.

## CROSS IN THE WOODS
### Indian River

Throughout this and many books like it, you'll find "The World's Largest This" or "That." It's not the size of the world's largest crucifix in Indian River, Michigan, that impresses, however; it's the aura about it. That aura is one reason that the cross has attracted millions of visitors of all faiths from around the world.

On June 26, 1946, the first Mass was celebrated at the newly established Indian River parish. The priest there got the idea to build an outdoor shrine after reading about the Blessed Kateri Tekakwitha. It was her practice to place crosses throughout the woods. The Indian maiden born in 1656 converted to Christianity at the age of eighteen. Her crosses were outdoor mini chapels for prayer. She was sort of the spiritual

*The world's largest crucifix, created by Michigan sculptor Marshall Fredericks, attracts visitors from all corners of the globe.*

Johnny Appleseed who gave Father Charles Brophy the idea for an outdoor shrine featuring a large wooden cross as the centerpiece.

In 1954 a 55-foot cross made of one redwood tree was erected. In 1959 a seven-ton bronze likeness of Jesus was added, making it the world's largest crucifix. Located just two minutes off I–75 at Exit 310, the cross was a popular stop for tourists heading up to the Upper Peninsula. In 1983 there was a complete renovation of the outdoor area including the altar, the Stations of the Cross, and the Shrine of the Madonna of the Highway. The grounds also include a shrine to St. Francis of Assisi, founder of the Franciscans, one of the largest orders in the Roman Catholic Church.

For the first fifty years of the shrine's existence, any extended stay was possible only during the spring-through-fall seasons because the location in Michigan's northern snow belt made midwinter visits impossible. That problem was rectified on June 29, 1997, when the new church was dedicated; now visitors can spend time at the cross 365 days a year. There are daily services inside the church year-round and outdoor services in summer.

You'll find the Cross in the Woods at 7078 M68. Contact (213) 238–8973 or www.rc.net/gaylord/crossinwoods.

## S I S T E R S   W H O   A R E   H A B I T   F O R M I N G
### *Indian River*

I t's 8:00 A.M. and 525 sisters are faithfully lined up, properly attired in starched collars, and ready to meet their adoring public. Sshh . . . silence is the golden rule here. Not a sound is uttered as they all conduct themselves as perfect dolls. The doors are opening for the day at the Nun Doll Museum.

*The habits of 525 religious orders in both North and South America grace the halls of the Nun Doll Museum.*

"Michigan's best-kept secret" started as a private collection. You might think it belonged to a modest Catholic girl aspiring to one day enter the convent . . . but instead it was Sally Rogalski, a young Lutheran, who came up with the idea of dressing her dolls as nuns in thanksgiving for the life-saving care her mother had received from the Daughters of Charity.

Sally converted, married, and her hobby grew into a habit she just couldn't kick. In 1967, out of gratitude for additional favors received, she and her late husband, Wally, decided to present a few of the dolls to Indian River's Cross in the Woods. Today there are hundreds of them, some even life sized, representing the detailed garb of religious orders the world over, many dressed by the nuns themselves. In 1988 Pope John Paul II issued an official proclamation recognizing the Rogalskis and their Nun Doll Museum as the largest such collection anywhere.

And since confession is good for the soul, it's time to 'fess up. There aren't 525 sisters. Included in that number is a priest in his robes, because, as Sally says, "He should be there."

The Nun Doll Museum is open daily from 8:00 A.M. to 6:00 P.M. The Rogalskis have stated that there will never be a charge for admission. It's located on M68, Exit 310 off I-75. For more info, call (231) 238-8973.

## *If You Build It, They Will Come*
### *Mackinaw City*

J. C. Stilwell of Mackinaw City was a young punk—that's an apprentice ironworker— when he became part of the 2,000-man team brought together in 1954 to construct the Mackinac Bridge. Lots of "team building" went on, sometimes twenty-four hours a day.

Take the winter's night that Curly Olsen and a twenty-seven-year-old Stilwell hiked the 3-mile catwalk between Piers 22 and 17, guided only by a fifth of whiskey. Suspended 500 feet in the air, "We were the only ones stupid enough to do it."

The balanced blend of hard work and carousing produced durable bonds of friendship among the "finest men in the world." Which is why, in 1980, Stilwell erected the Mackinac Bridge Museum.

What began as a few torn-off covers of magazines has snowballed into a major "Shrine to the Ironworkers," with contributions from members all over the country. The highlight is a

*Autographed hard hats worn by bridge workers*
*adorn the ceiling of the Mackinac Bridge*
*Museum, including that of museum founder*
*J. C. Stilwell.*

continuously running thirty-minute video, with actual footage of the toil and tear these young men sustained.

Stilwell promises to display any authentic "Mighty Mac" memorabilia that people send. A man true to his word, an urn enclosed with a share of the ashes of head steward Ray Haugh fulfills half of a pledge made years ago. The waters off Tower 20 handled the other half.

Be sure to look up above at the suspension of hard hats, all signed by their original owners. Mustered in the middle is a lone pair of roller skates identified as belonging to Mike Hornick, who, whenever the "spirits" moved him, used them to get to work on the bridge.

The Mackinaw Bridge Museum occupies the top floor of Stilwell's Mama Mia Pizzeria at 231 East Central. It's open May 1 through October 30, 8:00 A.M. to midnight. Free admission. Phone (231) 436–5534.

## STILL LIFE IN JURASSIC PARK
### Ossineke

*D*inosaurs were hip and cool in Ossineke long before that larger-than-life purple "I love you—you love me" Barney was even a glimmer in his parents' carnivorous eye. Paul Domke, back in 1934, for some unknown reason fell under the spell of the giant terrestrials. Once hooked, he stopped at nothing to share his fascination with the rest of Michigan.

From his own home-brewed recipe, he sculpted dinosaurs with life-sized dimensions and didn't stop for the next forty years, until twenty-six had been meticulously crafted. Not just mammoth outlines, each creature is prehistorically correct right down to the muscular tendons.

With a vision of engaging the public with *Tyrannosaurus rex* and iguanodon, Dinosaur Gardens Prehistorical Zoo was created—forty eerie acres of swampy land a la *Jurassic Park*.

Here's a chance to get up-close and personal with the big boys, even exploring the guts inside. Those inviting steps coming out of the apotosaurus's side take you on a journey of discovery to find, instead of the heart, a figure of Jesus. Is it any coincidence that the body of running water here is "Devil River"?

Whatever you conclude, it's a thought-provoking mile-long hike that weaves you through the towering four-legged beasts with titillating tidbits: Did you know that the stegosaurus had two brains, one—the size of a walnut—to operate his jaws and front legs, and the other, twenty times larger, controlling the action of his backside? I think we all know someone who similarly has predominant intelligence in the posterior.

Dinosaur Gardens and its reproductions in the prehistorical zoo are located 10 miles south of Alpena on U.S Highway 23. It's open seven days a week: from Memorial Day through Labor Day 10:00 A.M. to 8:00 P.M., and in May and September until 4:00 P.M. Call (517) 471–5477 or (877) 823–2408. Admission charge. The reproduction disclaimer part is more important than you may realize . . . in 1987 one man asked for his money back, disappointed that the dinosaurs weren't real.

## "BUT OFFICER, THIS IS THE FIRST TIME I'VE . . ."

*Roscommon*

On May 29, 2002, at approximately 4:20 P.M. in Roscommon County, the unthinkable befell one unsuspecting motorist. After more than thirty years behind the wheel, Bryan Allen Becker of Oakland County was issued his very first one-in-a-million-mile speeding ticket. Not just his first for zipping up I–75 at a 75 mph clip; no, this was his only violation of any kind . . . ever. While this may not seem particularly noteworthy, several reasons validate this story's inclusion.

1. When Becker called the 83rd District Court to learn the fate of his fine at 4:28 P.M. that same day, a friendly recording answered, informing jurors that all cases for May 9 had been settled. Proceedings would next be scheduled the week of May 16. I guess they believe in giving jurists as much advance notice as possible, although eleven months seems to be stretching it.

2. Further examination revealed that the most prominent speed trap in the state is along I–75 near West Branch. Roscommon runs a close second.

3. State Trooper Keith McCauley, now retired, gained celebrity status in the 1990s for writing more tickets than anyone else. His typical day in Ogemaw County consisted of signing his autograph on twenty-five to thirty numbered, limited edition pieces of paper. According to his buddies, "all of them were good . . . he hardly ever went to court."

4. Unaware that life is moving faster these days, troopers currently hand out on a daily basis something much less, generally around three or four, but that number can go as high as fifteen on weekends when they say "it's like shooting fish in a barrel."

5. And lastly, the stark reality is that Bryan is my once flawless husband, who now has proved he'll do anything in the pursuit of a good scoop.

# THE HEART OF HIS FANS: FROM SCREAMIN' TO STREAMIN'

*I*n the 1960s Alpena High School graduate Donny Hartman was living his dream life. An enthusiastic teen,
strumming a guitar with the Chevelles during the height
of the rock 'n' roll craze, he managed to travel more than
100,000 miles a year and never leave the state.

Then, as a member of the hottest warm-up group in
the country, The Frost, his travels took him much farther,
including appearances on the bill with Three Dog Night,
Led Zeppelin, Eric Clapton, the Moody Blues, Fleetwood
Mac, and B. B. King. His star continued to rise: The band
sold 50,000 albums in two days in Detroit, becoming the
only act to sell out both Cobo Hall and Olympia Stadium.

But ever since he was a wee tyke, there was a quieter sound calling him . . . the sound of a fish biting at the end of the line. So Hartman gave it his all, working five nights a week making music until 2:00 in the morning, when he'd put down his guitar and pick up his rod and reel to be out on the lakes before the crack of dawn.

Victorious as the champion of several local bass tournaments, he racked up some pretty big catches: a 5½-pound smallmouth bass (during fall season), 6½-pound largemouth bass, 13-pound walleye, 30-pound pike, and, in Alaska, a 146-pound halibut, while fooling around for, well, just the halibut. Yet as a "semipro" fisherman, a shortage of money kept him out of the "reely" big time.

Living proof that you can always do what you love to do, by night Hartman continues to write and sing the blues, releasing his own CD Famous in Most Places and playing clubs statewide with the Donny Hartman Band. By day he's a fishing guide, treating optimistic anglers to his expertise with the waterways around Rogers City, in the northeastern portion of the Lower Peninsula. You'll know him when you see him . . . inscribed on the side of his boat are two words that sum it up best: FISHIN' MUSICIAN.

You can catch up with Donny Hartman on Fletcher's Floodwater at Jack's Landing in Hillman, (989) 742–4370; or at his Web site, www.donnyhartmanband. com.

Make sure you have the word band in there. If you just enter Donny Hartman, you get two guys drinking Heinekens.

## THINGS GO BETTER WITH . . . BILL HICKS!

### Sparr

Travel just 5 miles outside Gaylord down a quiet dirt road and you'll find "the real thing." The sign outside reads THE BOTTLE CAP MUSEUM. Yet it's so much more than the name implies. Enter the door of Bill Hicks's 7,000-square-foot home and you'll see an exhibit of Coca-Cola memorabilia rivaled by none. In fact, Bill boasts the largest collection on public display in all of Michigan.

His passion for anything Coke began about thirty years ago when he owned a hunting lodge. While he was picking up "trash" from the grounds, someone saw him throwing away an old Coke bottle. The stranger told him it was worth $5.00. Since Bill, by his own admission, loves money, that's all he needed to hear to convince him to keep it.

Today he has more than 5,000 items. Wearing his favorite collectible, a 1930s tour guide hat, he'll walk you through the entire assemblage while you enjoy the history of Coke with his colorful commentary. A true Coke historian, he'll tell you everything you've ever wanted to know about the beverage and then some. Did you know the company has had 436 different slogans since 1886?

Rows of bottles line the walls from floor to ceiling, the oldest dating back to 1894. Every nook and cranny is filled with some fun remembrance of Coke. It may be a hallway filled with fourteen different picnic baskets, a wall packed with forty different clocks, or a case filled with curiosities, such as a 1950 musical cigarette lighter.

It's not just the items that make this product dedication mind-boggling. It's the way each piece is presented. Hicks has

*An expert Coca-Cola historian, Bill Hicks wears his love of the soft drink on his head, his heart, and every inch of his homegrown museum.*

created impressive scenes, like the Christmas room stocked with the artistry of Coke's original Santa Claus. When he needed something special to showcase the wide variety of pieces, he simply handcrafted all his own display cases. As he says, "I'm a jack of all trades and a master of them all."

Bill's Bottle Cap Museum is technically open Wednesday through Saturday, 11:00 A.M. to 5:00 P.M., but he never says no to anyone who wants a tour whenever they call. The number is (989) 732–1931, and the museum is located at 4944 Sparr Road. Admission charge. A glass full of Coca-Cola is included.

There's just one stipulation . . . in Hicks's home, "you never say the P word."

# INDEX

# ABOUT THE AUTHORS

Colleen Burcar has worked in radio, television, and newspapers for many years. Thirteen of those years were spent working alongside Gene Taylor. She now works in media consulting and public relations and her voice continues to be heard on commercials across the country. The mother of a daughter, Kimberly, Colleen currently resides in suburban Detroit with her husband, Bryan Becker, and toy poodle, Chloe.

Gene Taylor was an Emmy Award–winning entertainer, writer, and producer. His nearly twenty-year collaboration with Detroit radio legend Dick Purtan included serving as writer and executive producer of the popular *Dick Purtan & Purtan's People* morning show on Detroit's Oldies 104.3 (WOMC). Gene was probably best known for the numerous characters that he created and voiced for the show, but beyond his radio work, Gene was also involved with a number of charitable organizations, including the Salvation Army.

# IN MEMORIAM

*"My Most Unforgettable Character"*

**R**eader's Digest magazine has a monthly column called "My Most Unforgettable Character." In my life, and I'm sure in many others, Gene Taylor would be at the top of the list; and it would be a long distance before you would find a second person.

Gene was first and foremost a student of life. He lived life to the fullest, and was amazed at both its complexity and simplicity. He would frequent both the "greasy spoon" restaurants and the five-star continental cuisine palaces of every city he visited.

He was well read. He devoured books, newspapers, magazines, the latest movies and TV shows. He knew the latest in everything, and he enjoyed dressing with flair! From his signature bow ties, royal purple blazer, and bowler hat with driving gloves, to his World Wrestling Federation T-shirt, Gene could pull it off. He even carried a jar of Grey Poupon mustard in the glove box of his 1957 Ford Thunderbird. Just in case someone asked.

No one I have ever met packed as much into the fifty-three years God gave him as he did.

Gene was always asking questions, and the more offbeat the subject, the more interested he would become. As may be recounted in this book, Gene was as comfortable being with the chairman of the board of one of the Big Three auto companies as he was serving a cup of soup, a sandwich, and a piece of fruit to a homeless person off the Salvation Army Bed and Bread truck every Wednesday afternoon on the streets of Detroit.

I don't think Gene Taylor ever had a bad day. There was always someone to talk to, something to learn, someone to help.

Gene was responsible for motivating people to achieve their goals and dreams, and sometimes would make a phone call to help another get a job.

Gene was funny, compassionate, inquisitive, humane, and loving to all.

Detroit radio personality Dick Purtan probably said it best in Gene's eulogy: "If Gene Taylor isn't in heaven right now, none of us have a chance in hell to get there ourselves."

—Mark "Doc" Andrews, sports director, WOMC-FM

### Remembering Dad

**W**hat can you say about a person like Gene Taylor? Most people will focus on his charity work with the Salvation Army or his quick wit and career with Dick Purtan. But Gene Taylor is just Dad to me. Not that his comedy or generosity were not a part of it, because they were, but to me he was so much more than that. At his funeral I did not get up and speak. My brother Kelly got up and spoke for both of us. So now it is my turn to speak for both of us.

Since I was an infant my parents have been divorced; Dad lived in Detroit and I lived in Toronto. Every three weeks he would drive up after work to pick my brother and me up and then drive back to Detroit. This would sometimes take up to ten hours after waking up at 3:30 A.M. and going to work. However, he was still delighted to see us, and we'd talk all the way back. As a kid I don't think that I was fully aware of what his job was and how he affected so many people each day by putting a smile on their faces, either through the radio or in person.

The things I loved about Dad the most were things the general public never saw; maybe that's what made them so special. Dad loved James Bond and Mafia movies, and the day after he saw one he would either be Gene "No Nose" Petrachelli or Bond, Gene Bond. Dad also had some tricks up his sleeve for when I was being a "teenager." Whenever he suspected that I was lying, he would calmly take my hand and tell me that he could tell if I was lying by my heartbeat, which he would feel through my thumb. I don't know why, but it worked every time. . . possibly because every time I was lying, but that's beside the point. It must have been the straight face that he struggled to make but I would just burst out laughing and admit everything. Another method he used was the "tickilator." When I was trying to be mad and prove a point, he would tickle me till I had tears in my eyes. He would also use the "tickilator" when I would ambush him while he was napping—I had to get back at him somehow—he would wake up and I'd get one good hit with a pillow in before the tickle tears welled up. Looking back, these little silly things were what made him great to me.

Dad always said that travel was the best education. We had some amazing trips to New York where we would walk through the city all night and just talk. When we went to Chicago for Easter we went to a couple of Second City shows, and Dad and I talked about the struggle it will be when I try to make in show business. The greatest talk we ever had about my future and career was one of the last times that he picked me up from Toronto. We spoke for at least two or three hours about what my plans for my future were. He was always there for me day and night no matter the problem. He was the best.

One of the special things about our relationship was that we kept each other grounded. When he would pick me up and I would complain about not having the latest gadget that I didn't need or not going to every party on the planet, he would put me back in my place. I did the same for him. Whenever we were in a fancy restaurant or store and he would be getting a little too elegant and overconfident, I would remind him that wrestling was on in twenty minutes and we'd race home. We would always bring each other back down to reality.

Despite the 250 miles that physically separated us, we would call each other every night and talk about our days. We would bounce ideas for school or work off each other. You would be surprised by how many Purtan scripts were originally my idea, but I never could have written them like he did. The greatest gift that Dad gave me was time. Even though we didn't live together, he was and is a huge part of my life. We are best friends and I miss him dearly, but every night before I go to sleep I talk to him about my day and bounce ideas off him . . . and even though he doesn't answer directly I know what he would say. He is the best dad anyone could ask for, and I am eternally grateful for every minute I spent with him.

—Chris and Kelly Taylor